THE

E	XPRESSIVE
A	ND
R	ECEPTIVE
L	ANGUAGE
I	NDIVIDUALIZATION

PROGRAM

VOLUME I

By

Lynne Mann

Illustrations by Claudia Rees   **Cover Design by Ernie Devane**

**HUMANICS
LEARNING**

Humanics Learning
PO Box 7400
Atlanta, GA 30357-0400

Copyright © 1982 Humanics Limited

Millennium Edition 1999

Library of Congress Card Catalog Number: 81-83048
ISBN 0-89334-067-7

TABLE OF CONTENTS

VERBS

HOUSE

FOODS

SEASONS

SPECIAL OCCASIONS

INTRODUCTION

The ultimate goal of the Expressive And Receptive Language Individualization or EARLI Program is to facilitate the child's efficient and appropriate use of verbal language. In order to achieve this goal, the EARLI Program has been designed in two sections: Receptive language (Volume I) and Expressive language (Volume II).

It is believed that before a child can use expressive language spontaneously, he must have had meaningful experiences to which verbal language has been attached. More simply, he must have receptive language. The Receptive portion of the EARLI Program encourages the child to develop and use receptive language. The enjoyable tasks it contains require the identification of linguistic concepts and vocabulary through non-verbal modes such as pointing and matching.

Once the child indicates an understanding of basic linguistic concepts and vocabulary, he can be expected to use verbal expressive language. The Expressive portion of the EARLI Program has been designed to provide varied experiences for the child to which he can attach verbal labels and names.

The EARLI Program provides the teacher with the flexibility of using one or both portions of the program depending on the needs of his or her students. Whether used in whole or in part, the EARLI Program is a supplemental language program which is appealing, enjoyable and simple to use.

HOW TO USE THE EARLI PROGRAM

The *Expressive And Receptive Language Individualization or EARLI Program* is composed of a series of lessons designed to facilitate the child's development of receptive language and use of expressive language. Each of the daily lessons includes an objective, a list of materials needed to implement the lesson, specific instructions for implementation, exit criteria for completion of the lesson, and illustrations to augment the lesson. The EARLI Program is designed to provide enjoyable daily language experiences to all children who will benefit from individualized attention to receptive and/or expressive language development.

Who should use the EARLI Program?

The EARLI Program has been designed to be used primarily, but not exclusively, by paraprofessionals (e.g., teacher's aides, parents, older students, volunteers). Because the EARLI Program does not require continual direction, intervention, or monitoring by the professional educator, the classroom teacher can plan constructive, independent use of the paraprofessional's time.

How should the EARLI Program be used?

The EARLI Program consists of a series of one hundred eighty-five different lessons which follow the natural sequence of language development. Approximately one-half the lessons (Volume I) are written to facilitate verbal receptive language. The other lessons (Volume II) are concerned with verbal expressive language. The unique construction of the Program allows the teacher to tailor use of the Program to meet the individual needs of a child. Some suggestions for use of the Program include:
1. Present all receptive lessons first and follow with all expressive lessons
2. Present one receptive lesson and follow with the corresponding expressive lesson
3. Present only receptive lessons
4. Present only expressive lessons

The lessons may be used with one child at a time or with a small group of two to four children. Each lesson is designed to last from ten to twenty minutes.

The EARLI Program is designed to meet the needs of individual children. The classroom teacher may use the EARLI Program to build a language enrichment program or as a rehabilitative language program. In either situation, use of the EARLI Program will augment the individual education plan for each child in a learning situation.

2

Guidelines for Using the Lessons

A. Before presenting a lesson:
   1. Always read through the day's lesson so that you will know what is expected.
   2. If lessons are being used with more than one child at a time, make sure that the appropriate number of each of the materials is available.
   3. Always make copies of the Lesson Illustrations. Again, if you are using the lessons with more than one child at a time, make sure you make the appropriate number of copies.
   4. Make sure that special materials are available when needed. Note that for Lessons R-68—R-75 and R-77—R-82 (Volume I) and Lessons E-51 and E-70 (Volume II), you will need certain foods. Be sure to read ahead and see that they are available.
   5. Obtain permission to take the children on walks or other excursions as suggested in some lessons.
   6. Make sure that each child has his own loose leaf notebook in which to keep his completed lessons and materials.

B. During the lesson:
   1. The object of the lesson is to give children experience with language. Make sure that the appropriate written and/or oral language is used.
   2. Allow time for the child(ren) to respond to the requests or instructions, keeping in mind that some children need more time than others.

C. When the lesson has been completed:
   1. Make sure the lessons and materials are placed in the child's notebook.
   2. Look at the lesson for the next day in order to prepare any special materials which might be needed.
   3. Try to have the notebooks accessible to the children. A child takes pride in his/her success and will enjoy re-doing some of the tasks.

Upon completion of the EARLI Program, each child will have a personalized, tangible, reusable notebook whch will serve two purposes: (a) to facilitate review of the language principles presented and (b) to facilitate future educational planning.

Materials and Supplies

Although most materials are listed for each lesson, the following comprehensive list will make organization easier. Most of the materials called for are found in every classroom, and it is suggested that they be readily available when presenting the lessons.

Loose leaf notebook for each child
Loose leaf paper, lined and unlined
Scissors
Index cards—3" × 5" and 5" × 8"

Color crayons
Markers
Adhesive tape
Paste/glue
Envelopes to hold index cards OR pocket dividers in notebook
Pencils
Erasers
Construction paper
Cardboard
Fabric scraps
Stapler
Magazines
Catalogues (Sears', Penneys', etc.)

Summary

The EARLI Program provides a sequential presentation of lessons designed to facilitate the development of receptive and expressive language. It is appealing to all young children and particularly beneficial to children with delayed verbal language. It is a program designed specifically, but not exclusively, for paraprofessional use without direction or intervention by the classroom teacher. The flexibility of the lesson presentation allows the Program to fit individual needs of the children using it. Each lesson is complete and includes an illustration or task to be completed by the child. Finally, the use of the EARLI Program will facilitate future educational planning.

SUGGESTED VOCABULARY LIST*

The following is a suggested vocabulary list from the John Tracy Clinic which represents vocabulary appropriate for the children of the age and at the language developmental level for which the EARLI Program was designed. This list encompasses the vocabulary words that will be presented throughout the EARLI Program lessons and can serve as a guide for the teacher in planning his or her use of the EARLI Program.

Nouns

Parts of the body:

ankle	eyelash	knee	toe
arm	face	leg	tongue
back	finger	lips	tooth
bones	foot/feet	mouth	thumb
body	forehead	muscle	waist
cheek	freckles	neck	wrist
chin	hair	nose	
ear	hand	shoulder	
elbow	head	skin	
eye	heel	stomach	

Clothes:

belt	jacket	ribbon	socks
blouse	jeans	robe	sweater
buckle	jumper	shirt	tie
button	nightgown	shoe	underpants
cap	pajamas	shoelace	undershirts
coat	pants	shorts	mittens
diaper	pin	skirt	ring
dress	pocket	slacks	umbrella
hat	raincoat	snap	watch
			zipper

*This list is part of the VOCABULARY LIST developed by the John Tracy Clinic, Los Angeles, California.

5

Shoes:

Boots
Rubbers
Sandals
Saddle Shoes
Tennis Shoes
Clogs

School and Desk Equipment:

blackboard	eraser	paint	scissors
cardboard	felt pen	paintbrush	stapler
chalk	finger paint	paper	string
chart	flannel board	paste	thumb tacks
clay	glue	pencil	
crayon	magnet	pen	
play dough	masking tape	rubber band	

Foods:

Cereal Products:

cereal	cream of wheat
hominy	
oatmeal	

Condiments:

garlic	pepper
jam	salt
ketchup	spice
mustard	sugar
paprika	

Dairy Products:

butter	ice cream
cheese	margarine
cream	milk
eggs	cottage cheese

Desserts:

apple brown betty
bread pudding
cake
candy
cookie
doughnuts

gingerbread
ice cream
ice cream cone
jello
pie
popsicle

pudding
sherbert
sundae
turnover

Drinks:

coffee
hot chocolate
cocoa
juice—
   apple
   grape
   grapefruit
   orange
   pineapple

kool-aid
lemonade
limeade
malt
milk
milkshake
pop—
   coca cola

Pepsi
root beer
Seven-up
ginger ale
punch
tea
tomato juice
water

Fruit:

apple
apricot
banana
blueberry
cherry
cranberry

grape
grapefruit
lemon
lime
melon—
   cantaloupe

honeydew
musk melon
  watermelon
orange
peach
pear

pineapple
plum
pomegranate
prune
raisins
strawberry
tangerine

Meat:

Beef:
ground beef
hamburger
meat ball
meat loaf
roast
steak
stew
liver
veal
hot dog

Fowl:
chicken
duck
goose
liver
turkey

Fish:
fish sticks
shrimp
tuna
crabs

Lamb:
chops

Pork:
bacon
ham
wiener

Vegetables:

asparagus	cabbage	peas
avacado	carrots	green pepper
beans—	cauliflower	pickle
green	celery	radish
lima	corn	salad
string	cucumber	spinach
baked	lettuce	squash
bean sprouts	okra	tomato
beet	onions	turnip
brussels sprouts	parsley	
broccoli		

Miscellaneous Foods:

applesauce	fritos	jelly	nuts
buns	gravy	lunchmeat	pancake
candy bar	gum	macaroni	pretzel
cold cuts	honey	marshmellow	rice
dough	ice	noodles	roll
flour			soup
spaghetti			
tortilla			
yogurt			

Grooming & Cleanliness:

bathtub	tissue
brush—	kleenex
tooth	toilet paper
hair	toothpaste
shoe polish	towel
shower	wash cloth
soap	comb

Houses-rooms:

attic	den	living room
bathroom	dining room	
breakfast	family room	
cellar	kitchen	

Mail:

address	invitation	name	stamp
card	letter	package	zip code
envelope	mailbox	post card	state

Money:

dime	quarter
dollar	nickel
half dollar	penny

Plants:

berry	leaf	stem
blossom	petal	
bud	roots	
bulb	seed	

Weather:

breeze	fog	rainbow	storm
cloud	foggy	snow	sunny
cloudy	frost	snowball	sunshine
dew	rain	snowflake	thunder
flood	rainy	snowman	windy

Shapes:

circle	round
line	square
oval	triangle
rectangle	

Time:

afternoon	hour	noon	week
date	minute	Spring	Winter
days of the week	month	Summer	year
evening	morning	today	yesterday
Fall	night	tomorrow	

Colors:

red	green	black
orange	blue	brown
yellow	purple	white

Environment:

school	street	hydrant	flower
house	car	stop light	stop sign
apartment	truck	tree	
store	bus	shrub/bush	

Animals:

cow	calf	bear	peacock
chicken	chick	elephant	porcupine
horse	colt	hippo	raccoon
pig	piglet	kangaroo	rhinoceros
sheep	lamb	leopard	seal
turkey	turkey chick	lion	tiger
duck	duckling	monkey	zebra

bird	frog	rabbit
cat	hamster	guinea pig
dog	mouse	turtle
fish	gerbil	

Adjectives:

above-below	broken-fixed	handsome-ugly	real-pretend
afraid-brave	bumpy-smooth	happy-sad	right-wrong
after-before	careful-careless	hard-soft	rough-smooth
alike-different	chilly-warm	heavy-light	sharp-dull
alive-dead	clean-dirty	here-there	side-front
all-none	close-far	high-low	short-tall
alone-together	cold-hot	huge-tiny	true-false
always-never	cool-warm	large-small	weak-strong
angry-calm	crooked-straight	later-sooner	well-sick
apart-together	dark-light	left-right	wild-tame
asleep-awake	deep-shallow	little-big	wonderful-awful
back-front	delicious-nasty	long-short	young-old
backward-forward	different-same	loose-tight	
bad-good	down-up	messy-neat	
bare-covered	dry-wet	middle-end	
beautiful-ugly	early-late	narrow-wide	
behind-in front	empty-full	naughty-nice	
bent-straight	far-near	new-old	
big-small	fast-slow	noisy-quiet	
bitter-sweet	fat-thin	over-under	
bottom-top	first-last	polite-rude	
bright-dull	funny-serious	quick-slow	

Conjunctions:

and	so
because	than
but	when
if	while
or	

Prepositions:

behind	far	on	up
beside	in	over	with
by	inside	to	
down	into	under	

Verbs:

answer	cough	go	like	push
ask	count	grab	listen	put
(be)	cry	grow	live	read
begin	cut	guess	lock	remember
behave	dance	hang up	lose	rest
bend	decorate	have	love	ride
bite	dig	hear	mail	roll
blink	do	help	make	run
blow	draw	hiccup	march	save
bother	drink	hide	measure	scare
break	drop	hit	melt	scratch
breathe	drive	hold	miss	scream
bring	dry	hop	mix	sell
bump	eat	hurry	move	see
bug	erase	hurt	need	sew
call	fall	jump	open	shake
carry	feed	keep	pat	share
catch	feel	kick	paint	shave
chew	fight	kiss	peel	shout
choose	find	kneel	pinch	shine
clap	finish	knock	play	sing
clean	fix	know	pop	sit
climb	fly	laugh	pound	skip
close	fold	learn	pour	slam
color	follow	leave	press	sleep
comb	forget	let	pretend	slide
come	get	lick	pull	slip
cook	give	lift	pump	smell

smile	start	tear	visit	wiggle
snap	step	tell	vomit	win
sneeze	stir	think	wait	wind
sniffle	stop	throw	walk	wink
spank	swallow	tie	want	wipe
spill	sweep	tickle	wash	wish
spin	swim	tiptoe	watch	work
spread	swing	touch	wear	wrap
squeeze	take	try	whisper	write
squirt	talk	turn	whine	yawn
stand	taste	twist	whistle	yell

THE EARLI PROGRAM: RECEPTIVE

Lesson R-1

Goal: To Recognize First Name and To Recognize Clothing Items By Color

Materials:

Unlined loose leaf paper	Scissors
Color crayons	Pins
Lesson Illustration	

Implementation:

1. Write or print your name on a piece of paper. Point from the written name to yourself, saying your name as the child looks at you.

2. Write or print the child's name below yours and say it as he looks at you. Point from the written name to the child as you say his name.

3. Cut the names apart and turn them over so you cannot see the print. Mix them up. Choose one and place it in front of the person it names (i.e., you or the child.)

4. Do the same for both names. Then give the child a turn to do both names. Help him if he is unsuccessful so he gets them matched to the correct person.

5. Pin the appropriate name on the child and on yourself.

6. Draw a picture of yourself (a stick figure will do) or use the appropriate Lesson Illustration.

7. Choose the color crayon that matches your hair color. Show the child that the colors are the same.

8. Color your hair on the picture.

9. Choose the color crayon that matches the color of one article of your clothing. Point out to the child that the colors match. Color the article of clothing on the picture.

10. Do the same for all articles of clothing you are wearing.

11. Draw a simple picture of the child (or use the appropriate Lesson Illustration) and repeat the coloring process, letting the child choose the appropriate color where he can.

12. When the child's picture is finished let him match the color crayons to the color clothing he has on and to the picture.

13. Place the pictures in the child's notebook.

Exit Criteria:

1. Child can choose his own name.
2. Child can match three colors to three items of his clothing.

Lesson R-2

Goal: To Choose Clothing Items Similar to Those The Child is Wearing

Materials:

Lesson Illustration (Make enough copies so that you can "clothe" yourself and the child)
Unlined loose leaf paper
Paste or glue
Scissors
Color crayons

Implementation:

1. Cut apart pictures of clothing items from the Lesson Illustration.
2. Show the child the pictures of clothing items, naming each as you show it to him.
3. Choose those items that you are wearing and paste them on a piece of paper one at a time (i.e., dress, shoes). Color them so they match yours.
4. When you've finished, draw your face, arms and legs. Print your name on the paper.
5. Let the child pick his clothing items from the pictures.
6. Let the child paste the items on the page and color the items appropriately.
7. Draw his face and label his picture with his name.
8. Place the picture in his notebook.

Exit Criteria:
Child must choose the correct clothing items, e.g., shoes, shirt, dress, pants, etc., which match his clothing.

PAJAMAS

RUBBERS

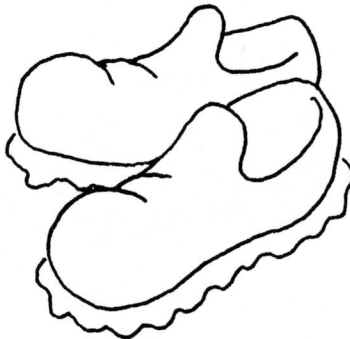

DRESS

COAT

HAT

UMBRELLA

DRESS

BOOTS

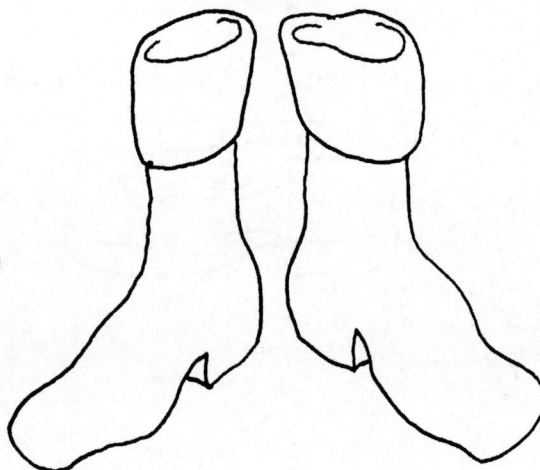

BRACELET

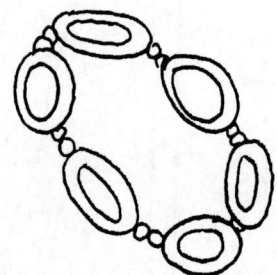

TIE

MITTENS

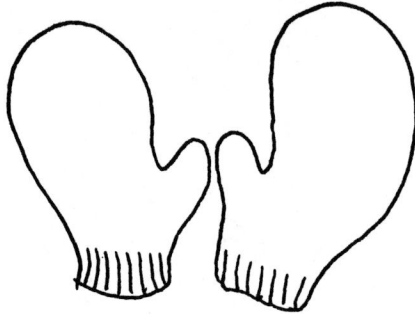

SOCKS

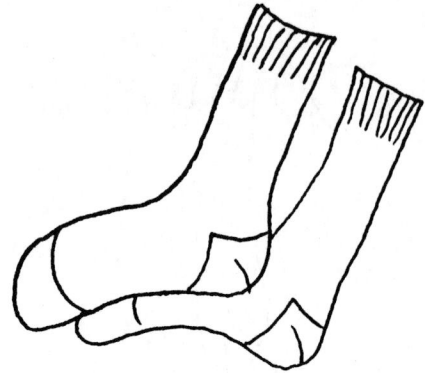

SKIRT

PANTS

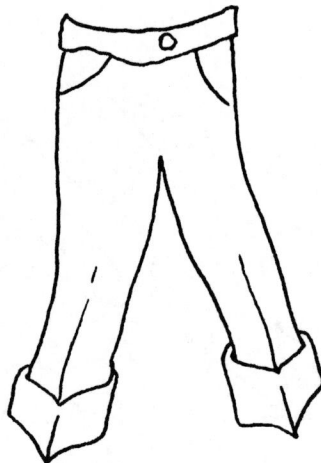

SWEATER

SHIRT

SHOES

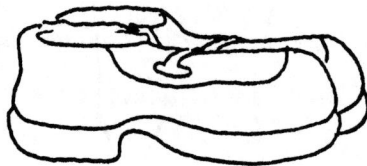

JACKET

TENNIS SHOES

SCARF

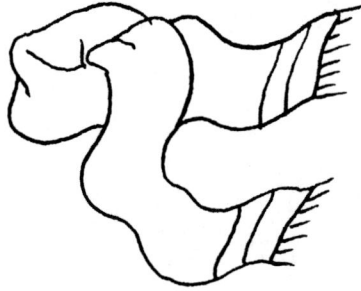

RAINCOAT + HAT

RINGS

GLOVES

BELT

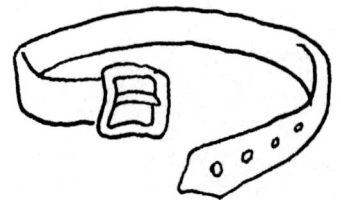

SHORTS

BLOUSE

CAP

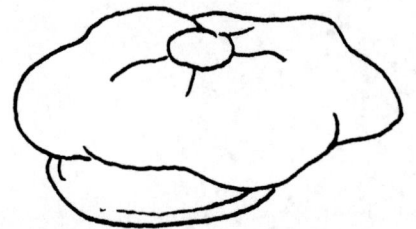

Lesson R-3

Goal: To Match Body Parts

Materials:

Lesson Illustration
Paste/glue
Unlined loose leaf paper

Implementation:

1. Copy each of the Lesson Illustrations and cut each one into body parts (i.e., arms, legs, torso, head, feet, hands).
2. Take the body parts one at a time and match them to yours. (For example, "Here's a hand, here's my hand.")
3. Put the pieces together to form a body.
4. Mix the parts up again and let the child match body parts to himself.
5. Have the child reassemble the body parts to form a body after he has matched each one to his own body.
6. Glue the pieces down to paper as child has reassembled them.
7. Place the picture in the child's notebook.

   Exit Criteria:
   The child is able to match the following body parts:
   Head
   Arms
   Hands
   Legs
   Feet

Lesson R-4

Goal: To Match Head Parts

Materials:

Lesson Illustration
Paste/glue
Scissors
Unlined loose leaf paper
Color crayons
Mirror (optional)

Implementation:

1. Cut apart the face picture. Place the pieces in a pile.
2. Choose one facial part. Match it to your own, naming it as you match it (for example, an eye)
3. (Optional) Show the child your eye in the mirror, your face and the picture.
4. Repeat steps 2 and 3 for three more pieces. Return them to the pile.
5. Let the child choose three pieces, one at a time, matching each to his own feature as you name it.
6. (Optional) Let him match the piece to his face in the mirror.
7. Repeat steps 2-6 for all the parts of the head and face.
8. Let the child reassemble the pieces.
9. Glue them onto a piece of paper.
10. Have the child color them according to his eye, hair and skin color.
11. Put the picture in the child's notebook.

Exit Criteria:
    Child must match all pieces to his facial parts:

Hair	Cheeks
Ears	Chin
Eyes	Forehead
Nose	Eyebrows
Mouth	

Lesson R-5

Goal: To Recognize Objects in Classroom

Materials:

Lesson Illustration.
Crayons
Pencils
Loose leaf paper (about 10 sheets)
Paste/glue
Scissors
Catalogue (Sears', Penneys', etc.)

Implementation:

1. Choose one of the pictured items from the Lesson Illustration and have the child match it to an object in the room as you name it. (Example, "That's a table. Find our table.")
2. Continue for all items possible.
3. Let the child find a picture in the catalogue of an item in the classroom.
4. Paste each Lesson Illustration and each picture from the catalogue on a sheet of paper, and label it.
5. Color the illustrations appropriately if time permits.
6. Place the papers in the child's notebook.

   Exit Criteria:
      Child must match at least the following items to the pictures:
         Desk/table
         Chair
         Blackboard

BLACKBOARD

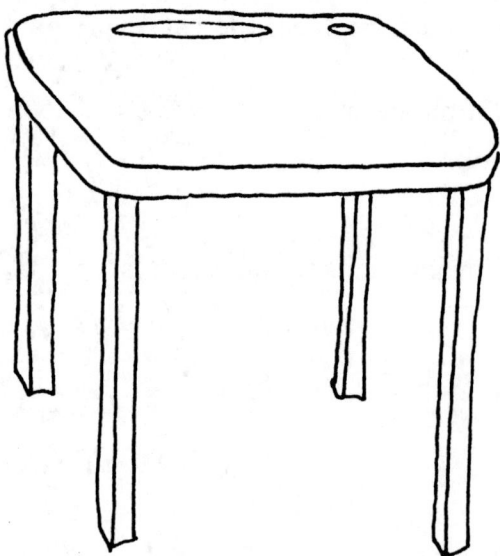

DESK

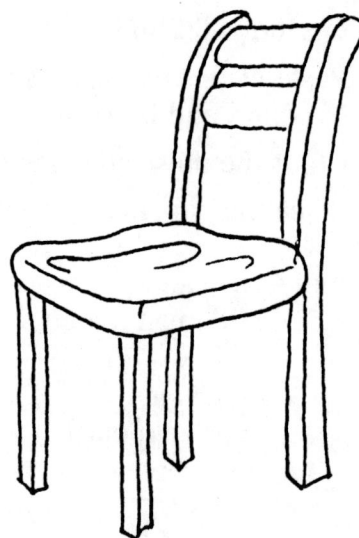

CHAIR

ERASER

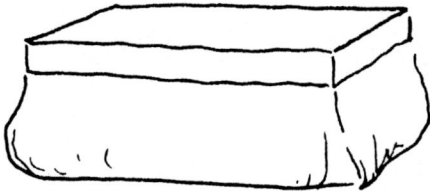

CHALK

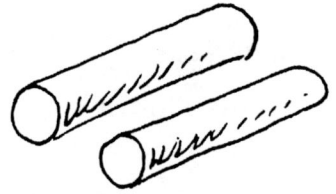

PENCIL

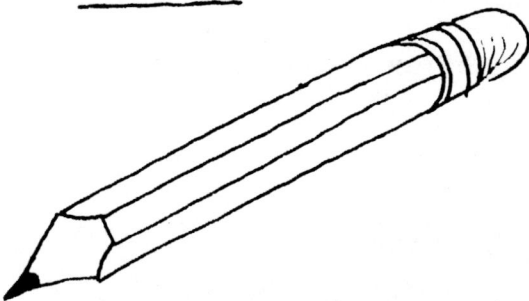

CRAYONS

BOOKS

PAPER

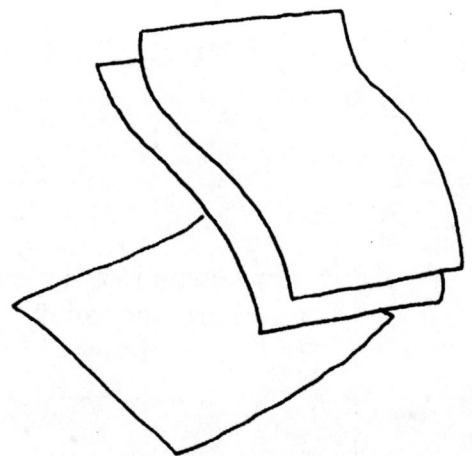

Lesson R-6

Goal: To Recognize Neighborhood Structures

Materials:

Lesson Illustration
Unlined loose leaf paper
Paste/glue
Scissors
Pencils

Implementation:

1. Take a brief walk around the school and point out to the child what can be seen. (For example, "That is a bush. That is a car.")
2. Go back to the classroom and find pictures in the Lesson Illustration to match what you saw on your walk.
3. Name each item as the child points to it.
4. Cut out each item the child points out.
5. Paste the items on a piece of paper. Color each appropriately.
6. Take the papers back outside and have the child identify each pictured item.
7. Return to the classroom and place the papers in the child's notebook.

Exit Criteria:
Child matches the following items:

School	Playground or play yard
Car	People
Tree/bush	House/apartment
Street	

Note: For Lesson R-7, the teacher should have photographs of the child, his family members and family pets, and should know their names and, with respect to siblings, their ages.

SCHOOL

GROCERY

Lesson R-7

Goal: To Recognize Family Members

Materials:

Lesson Illustrations, as needed
Photographs of family members
Color crayons
Paper

Implementation:

1. Show the child photographs (if available) or Lesson Illustrations of family members naming each as you show them.
2. Let the child color the Lesson Illustration of each family member appropriately.
3. Let the child draw a picture of his family.
4. Label and match each member in the child's picture to the photograph.
5. Put photographs, Lesson Illustrations and child's picture into the notebook.

Exit Criteria:
    Child can draw picture of self or family members.

Note: For Lesson R-8, the teacher will need the Peabody Language Development Kit.

36

Lesson R-8

Goal: To Recognize Clothing Items By Who Wears Them

Materials:

Boy & girl silhouettes and clothing from the Peabody Language Development Kit
Catalogue (Sears', Penneys', etc.)
Paste/glue
Scissors
Loose leaf paper

Implementation:

1. Look through the catalogue and cut out pictures of clothing items as the child points to them.
2. Have child separate boy's clothing from girl's clothing as you name them.
3. Label one sheet "BOYS" and one sheet "GIRLS." Paste clothing items on the appropriate sheet.
4. Label all clothing items on sheets.
5. Insert sheets in child's notebook.
6. When using the PLDK, have the child dress the dolls in appropriate clothing.

Exit Criteria:
    Child must separate boys' clothing from girls'.

Lesson R-9

Goal: To Recognize Farm Animals

Materials:

Two copies of Lesson Illustration R-9
Lesson Illustration R-13 (farm background)
Envelope
Paste/glue

Implementation:

1. Cut apart the pictures of farm animals in both copies of Lesson Illustration R-9.
2. Show the child the picture of the farm. Name and label it.
3. One at a time, show the child one set of the pictures of the animals, naming each one as you show it to him.
4. Take out the second picture of each animal and have the child match it to the first picture. Help the child name each animal as he matches the pictures.
5. After all the pictures have been matched, mix them up and lay them face down on a table or other flat surface.
6. Play "Concentration." Have the child turn over one picture. Help him name the animal picture. Then have the child turn over another picture, trying to find the matching picture. If he is successful, set aside the matched pair. If he is not, have him put both pictures back in place, face down.
7. Take turns with the child playing the game until all the pictures are matched.
8. Paste one set of animal pictures on the picture of the farm.
9. If time permits, color the picture.
10. Put the farm picture in the child's notebook.
11. Put the other set of animal pictures in an envelope and store the envelope in the child's notebook for later use.

Exit Criteria:
Child is able to match all animal pictures.

Lesson R-10

Goal: To Match Adult and Baby Animals

Materials:

Lesson Illustration R-10
Picture of farm from Lesson R-9
Paste/glue
Loose leaf paper
Pencil
Color crayons

Implementation:

1. Cut apart the pictures of animals in Lesson Illustration R-10.
2. Show the child the picture of the farm from Lesson R-9, naming the farm and each of the animals pasted on the picture.
3. Show the child the loose pictures of the adult farm animals, naming each one as you show it to him. (For example, "This is a cow." "This is a chicken.")
4. Show the child the pictures of the baby animals one by one, naming each one as you show it to him.
5. Match each adult to its baby.
6. Mix the pictures up and let the child match the adult animals to their babies.
7. You may want to play Concentration matching baby animals to adults.
8. Paste each pair of pictures to a piece of paper. Label each animal and baby.
9. If time permits, color the pictures.
10. Put the papers in the child's notebook.

Exit Criteria:
The child can match adult animals to babies.

48

Lesson R-11

Goal: To Recognize Zoo Animals

Materials:

Two copies of Lesson Illustration R-11
Lesson Illustration R-13 (zoo background)
Envelope
Paste/glue
Color crayons

Implementation:

1. Cut apart the pictures of the animals in both copies of Lesson Illustration R-11.
2. Show the child the picture of the zoo. Name and label it.
3. One at a time, show the child one set of the pictures of the animals, naming each one as you show it to him.
4. Take out the second picture of each animal and have the child match it to the first picture. Help the child name each animal as he matches the pictures.
5. After all the pictures have been matched, mix them up and lay them face down on a table or other flat surface.
6. Play "Concentration" with the child until all the pictures are matched. As each picture is turned over, name the animal pictured.
7. Paste one set of zoo animals onto the zoo picture.
8. If time permits, color the picture.
9. Put the zoo picture in the child's notebook.
10. Put the remaining set of animal pictures in an envelope and store the envelope in the child's notebook for later use.

Exit Criteria:
The child is able to match all fifteen pictures.

BEAR

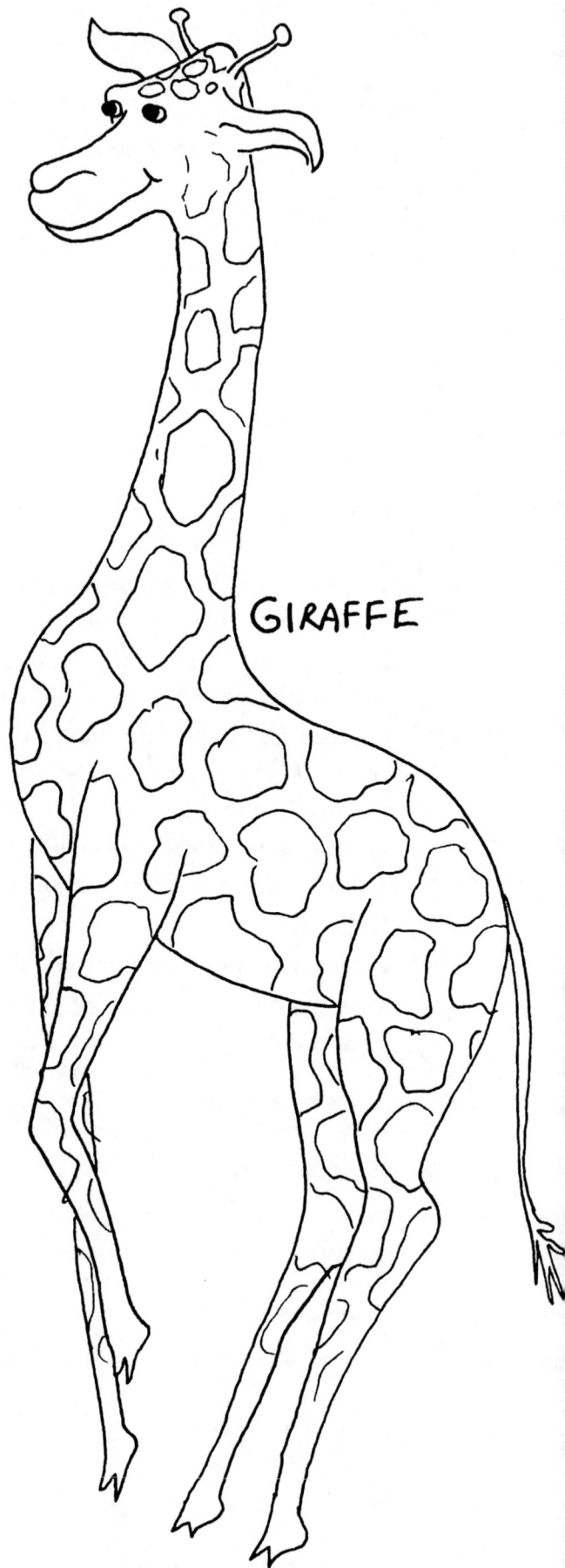

GIRAFFE

ELEPHANT

50

HIPPOPOTAMUS

KANGAROO

MONKEY

51

LION

PEACOCK

LEOPARD

PORCUPINE

RACOON

RHINOSCEROS

SEAL

TIGER

ZEBRA

Lesson R-12

Goal: To Recognize Domestic Animals

Materials:

Two copies of Lesson Illustration R-12
Lesson Illustration R-13 (pet store background)
Paste/glue
Envelope
Color crayons

Implementation:

1. Cut apart the pictures of pets in both copies of Lesson Illustration R-12.
2. Show the child the picture of the pet store. Name and label it.
3. One at a time, show the child one set of the pictures of the animals, naming each one as you show it to him.
4. Take out the second picture of each animal and have the child match it to the first picture. Help the child name each animal as he matches the pictures.
5. After all the pictures are matched, mix them up and place them face down on a table or other flat surface.
6. Play "Concentration" with the child until all the pictures have been matched. As each picture is turned over, name the animal pictured.
7. Paste one set of animals onto the pet store background.
8. If time permits, color the picture.
9. Put the pet store picture in the child's notebook.
10. Put the remaining set of animal pictures in an envelope and store the envelope in the child's notebook for later use.

Exit Criteria:
The child is able to match all eleven pictures.

RABBIT

CAT

BIRD

FISH

HAMSTER

DOG

GERBIL

MOUSE

TURTLE

FROG

GUINEA
PIG

Lesson R-13

Goal: To Discriminate Between Farm, Zoo and Domestic Animals

Materials:

Three envelopes of animal pictures (farm, zoo and domestic) from Lessons R-9, R-11 and R-12
Three pictures of backgrounds (farm, zoo and pet store) (Lesson Illustration R-13)
Color crayons

Implementation:

1. Lay the three background pictures in front of the child. Name and label each one.
2. Take all the pictures from the envelopes, mix them up and lay them face down on a table or other flat surface.
3. Have the child pick up one picture at a time. As he turns the picture over, name the animal pictured and have the child place the picture on the appropriate background.
4. Continue until all the animals have been named and placed on the appropriate background.
5. It time permits, color the pictures.
6. Put the pictures and backgrounds into envelopes and put the envelopes in the child's notebook for later use.

   Exit Criteria:
   The child is able to place pictures of all the animals properly:

FARM	ZOO	PET STORE
cow	bear	bird
chicken	elephant	cat
horse	giraffe	dog
pig	hippo	fish
sheep	kangaroo	frog
turkey	leopard	hamster
duck	lion	mouse
dog	monkey	gerbil
frog	peacock	guinea pig
goat	porcupine	rabbit
	raccoon	turtle
	rhinoceros	
	seal	
	tiger	
	zebra	

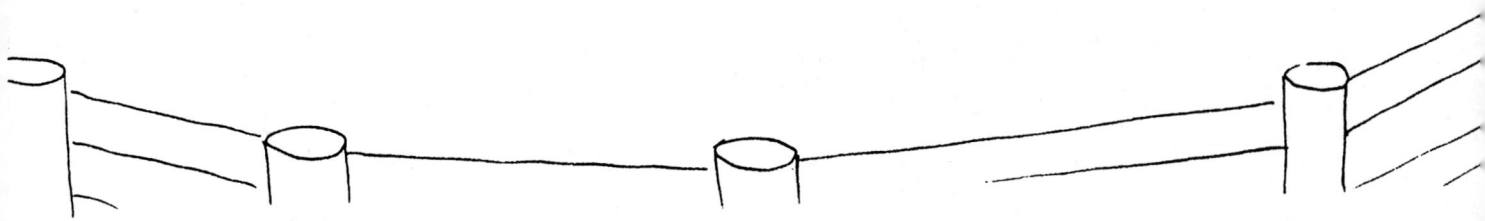

THE ZOO

Lesson R-14

Goal: To Match Colors: YELLOW

Materials:

Lesson Illustration R-14
Yellow color crayons
Yellow beads
Yellow paper
Yellow markers
Other yellow items that are available
Magazines
Scissors
Paste/glue
Loose leaf paper

Implementation:

1. Assemble several yellow items to use to acquaint the child with the concept of yellow. Name the yellow items one at a time. (For example, "This is a yellow crayon." "This is a yellow ball.")

2. Let the child find and gather together these and other yellow items in the room as you name them. (For example, "Find the yellow hat.")

3. Label a piece (or pieces) of loose leaf paper "YELLOW" with yellow crayon or marker.

4. Draw pictures of yellow items on the YELLOW paper. Name each item as you draw it and show the picture to the child.

5. Let the child cut and paste yellow paper onto the YELLOW page.

6. Let the child color with the yellow marker and crayon on the YELLOW page.

7. Look through magazines with the child for yellow pictures. Name the items pictured and cut them out as the child finds them.

8. Paste the pictures onto a sheet of yellow paper. Label each picture "YELLOW."

9. Put the papers in the child's notebook.

Exit Criteria:
    The child is able to recognize and choose three yellow items from a magazine.

Note: Lesson Illustration R-14 is to be used with Lessons R-14 through R-25. As you introduce the child to each color in Lessons R-14—R-22, color the appropriate space in the artist's palette, naming the color as you do. In Lessons R-23, R-24 and R-25, you may use the artist's palette to reinforce the child's knowledge of the colors and in matching exercises. (For example, have the child match his crayon to the appropriate space on the palette.)

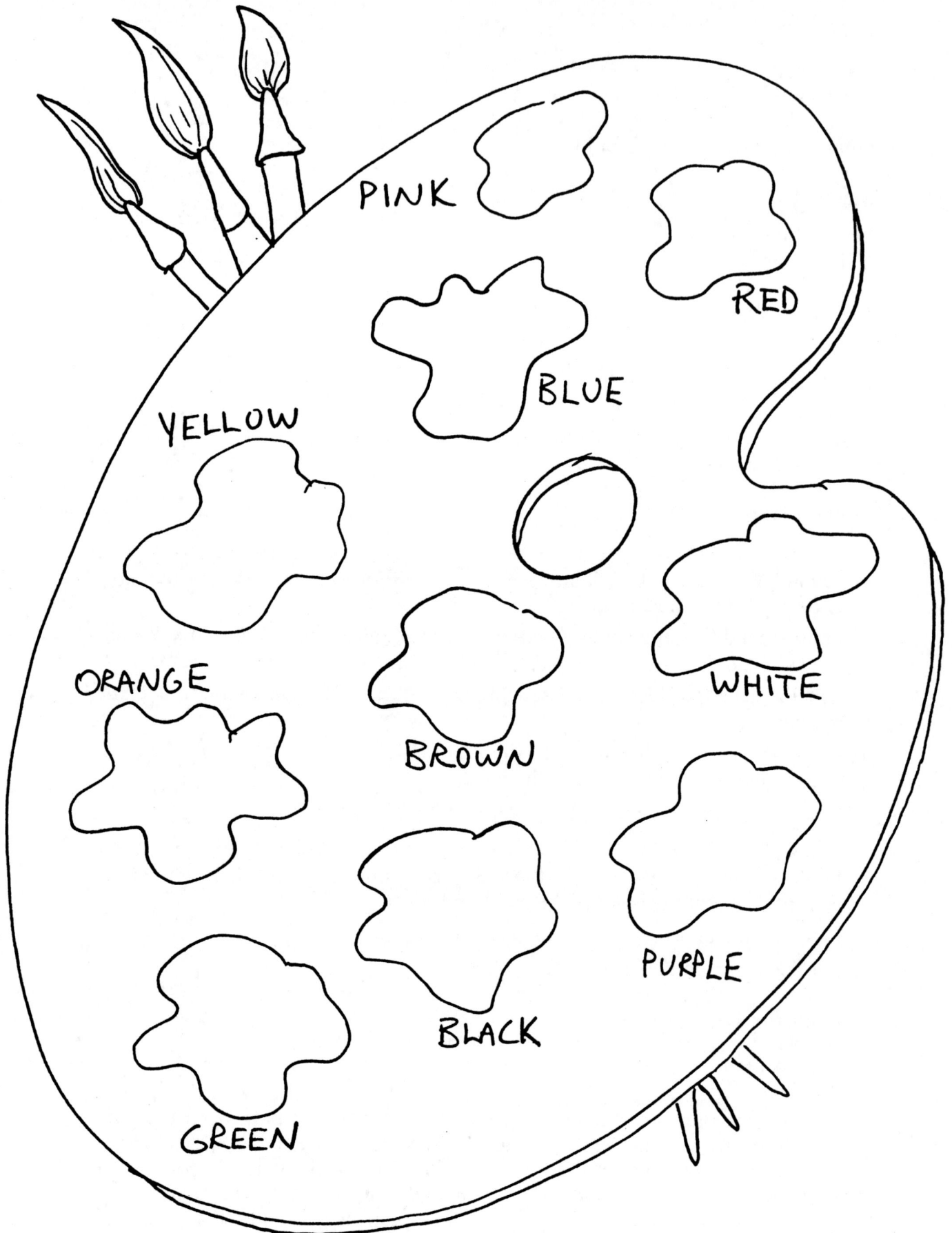

PINK

RED

BLUE

YELLOW

ORANGE

WHITE

BROWN

BLACK

PURPLE

GREEN

Lesson R-15

Goal: To Match Colors: ORANGE

Materials:

Lesson Illustration R-14
Orange color crayons
Orange beads
Orange paper
Orange markers
Other orange items that are available
Magazines
Scissors
Paste/glue
Loose leaf paper

Implementation:

1. Assemble several orange items to use to acquaint the child with the concept of orange. Name the orange items one at a time. (For example, "This is a orange crayon." "This is a orange ball.")
2. Let the child find and gather together these and other orange items in the room as you name them. (For example, "Find the orange hat.")
3. Label a piece (or pieces) of loose leaf paper "ORANGE" with orange crayon or marker.
4. Draw pictures of orange items on the ORANGE paper. Name each item as you draw it and show the picture to the child.
5. Let the child cut and paste orange paper onto the ORANGE page.
6. Let the child color with the orange marker and crayon on the ORANGE page.
7. Look through magazines with the child for orange pictures. Name the items pictured and cut them out as the child finds them.
8. Paste the pictures onto a sheet of orange paper. Label each picture "ORANGE."
9. Put the papers in the child's notebook.

Exit Criteria:
    The child is able to recognize and choose three orange items from a magazine.

Lesson R-16

Goal: To Match Colors: BLUE

Materials:

Lesson Illustration R-14
Blue color crayons
Blue beads
Blue paper
Blue markers
Other blue items that are available
Magazines
Scissors
Paste/glue
Loose leaf paper

Implementation:

1. Assemble several blue items to use to acquaint the child with the concept of blue. Name the blue items one at a time. (For example, "This is a blue crayon." "This is a blue ball.")
2. Let the child find and gather together these and other blue items in the room as you name them. (For example, "Find the blue hat.")
3. Label a piece (or pieces) of loose leaf paper "BLUE" with blue crayon or marker.
4. Draw pictures of blue items on the BLUE paper. Name each item as you draw it and show the picture to the child.
5. Let the child cut and paste blue paper onto the BLUE page.
6. Let the child color with the blue marker and crayon on the BLUE page.
7. Look through magazines with the child for blue pictures. Name the items pictured and cut them out as the child finds them.
8. Paste the pictures onto a sheet of blue paper. Label each picture "BLUE."
9. Put the papers in the child's notebook.

Exit Criteria:
   The child is able to recognize and choose three blue items from a magazine.

Lesson R-17

Goal: To Match Colors: RED

Materials:

Lesson Illustration R-14
Red color crayons
Red beads
Red paper
Red markers
Other red items that are available
Magazines
Scissors
Paste/glue
Loose leaf paper

Implementation:

1. Assemble several red items to use to acquaint the child with the concept of red. Name the red items one at a time. (For example, "This is a red crayon." "This is a red ball.")
2. Let the child find and gather together these and other red items in the room as you name them. (For example, "Find the red hat.")
3. Label a piece (or pieces) of loose leaf paper "RED" with red crayon or marker.

4. Draw pictures of red items on the RED paper. Name each item as you draw it and show the picture to the child.
5. Let the child cut and paste red paper onto the RED page.
6. Let the child color with the red marker and crayon on the RED page.
7. Look through magazines with the child for red pictures. Name the items pictured and cut them out as the child finds them.
8. Paste the pictures onto a sheet of red paper. Label each picture "RED."
9. Put the papers in the child's notebook.

Exit Criteria:
The child is able to recognize and choose three red items from a magazine.

Lesson R-18

Goal: To Match Colors: GREEN

Materials:

Lesson Illustration R-14
Green color crayons
Green beads
Green paper
Green markers
Other green items that are available
Magazines
Scissors
Paste/glue
Loose leaf paper

Implementation·

1. Assemble several green items to use to acquaint the child with the concept of green. Name the green items one at a time. (For example, "This is a green crayon." "This is a green ball.")
2. Let the child find and gather together these and other green items in the room as you name them. (For example, "Find the green hat.")
3. Label a piece (or pieces) of loose leaf paper "GREEN" with green crayon or marker.
4. Draw pictures of green items on the GREEN paper. Name each item as you draw it and show the picture to the child.
5. Let the child cut and paste green paper onto the GREEN page.
6. Let the child color with the green marker and crayon on the GREEN page.
7. Look through magazines with the child for green pictures. Name the items pictured and cut them out as the child finds them.
8. Paste the pictures onto a sheet of green paper. Label each picture "GREEN."
9. Put the papers in the child's notebook.

Exit Criteria:
   The child is able to recognize and choose three green items from a magazine.

Lesson R-19

Goal: To Match Colors: PURPLE

Materials:

Lesson Illustration R-14
Purple color crayons
Purple beads
Purple paper
Purple markers
Other purple items that are available
Magazines
Scissors
Paste/glue
Loose leaf paper

Implementation:

1. Assemble several purple items to use to acquaint the child with the concept of purple. Name the purple items one at a time. (For example, "This is a purple crayon." "This is a purple ball.")
2. Let the child find and gather together these and other purple items in the room as you name them. (For example, "Find the purple hat.")
3. Label a piece (or pieces) of loose leaf paper "PURPLE" with purple crayon or marker.
4. Draw pictures of purple items on the PURPLE paper. Name each item as you draw it and show the picture to the child.
5. Let the child cut and paste purple paper onto the PURPLE page.
6. Let the child color with the purple marker and crayon on the PURPLE page.
7. Look through magazines with the child for purple pictures. Name the items pictured and cut them out as the child finds them.
8. Paste the pictures onto a sheet of purple paper. Label each picture "PURPLE."
9. Put the papers in the child's notebook.

Exit Criteria:
The child is able to recognize and choose three purple items from a magazine.

Lesson R-20

Goal: To Match Colors: BROWN

Materials:

Lesson Illustration R-14
Brown color crayons
Brown beads
Brown paper
Brown markers
Other brown items that are available
Magazines
Scissors
Paste/glue
Loose leaf paper

Implementation:

1. Assembly several brown items to use to acquaint the child with the concept of brown. Name the brown items one at a time. (For example, "This is a brown crayon." "This is a brown ball.")
2. Let the child find and gather together these and other brown items in the room as you name them. (For example, "Find the brown hat.")
3. Label a piece (or pieces) of loose leaf paper "BROWN" with brown crayon or marker.
4. Draw pictures of brown items on the BROWN paper. Name each item as you draw it and show the picture to the child.
5. Let the child cut and paste brown paper onto the BROWN page.
6. Let the child color with the brown marker and crayon on the BROWN page.
7. Look through magazines with the child for brown pictures. Name the items pictured and cut them out as the child finds them.
8. Paste the pictures onto a sheet of brown paper. Label each picture "BROWN."
9. Put the papers in the child's notebook.

Exit Criteria:
   The child is able to recognize and choose three brown items from a magazine.

Lesson R-21

Goal: To Match Colors: BLACK

Materials:

Lesson Illustration R-14
Black color crayons
Black beads
Black paper
Black markers
Other black items that are available
Magazines
Scissors
Paste/glue
Loose leaf paper

Implementation:

1. Assemble several black items to use to acquaint the child with the concept of black. Name the black items one at a time. (For example, "This is a black crayon." "This is a black ball.")
2. Let the child find and gather together these and other black items in the room as you name them. (For example, "Find the black hat.")
3. Label a piece (or pieces) of loose leaf paper "BLACK" with black crayon or marker.
4. Draw pictures of black items on the BLACK paper. Name each item as you draw it and show the picture to the child.
5. Let the child cut and paste black paper onto the BLACK page.
6. Let the child color with the black marker and crayon on the BLACK page.
7. Look through magazines with the child for black pictures. Name the items pictured and cut them out as the child finds them.
8. Paste the pictures onto a sheet of black paper. Label each picture "BLACK."
9. Put the papers in the child's notebook.

Exit Criteria:
   The child is able to recognize and choose three black items from a magazine.

Lesson R-22

Goal: To Match Colors: WHITE

Materials:

Lesson Illustration R-14
White color crayons
White beads
White paper
White markers
Other white items that are available
Magazines
Scissors
Paste/glue
Loose leaf paper

Implementation:

1. Assemble several white items to use to acquaint the child with the concept of white. Name the white items one at a time. (For example, "This is a white crayon." "This is a white ball.")

2. Let the child find and gather together these and other white items in the room as you name them. (For example, "Find the white hat.")

3. Label a piece (or pieces) of loose leaf paper "WHITE" with white crayon or marker. (Use colored paper if necessary for the lettering to show up.)

4. Draw pictures of white items on the WHITE paper. Name each item as you draw it and show the picture to the child.

5. Let the child cut and paste white paper onto the WHITE page.

6. Let the child color with the white marker and crayon on the WHITE page.

7. Look through magazines with the child for white pictures. Name the items pictured and cut them out as the child finds them.

8. Paste the pictures onto a sheet of white paper. Label each picture "WHITE."

9. Put the papers in the child's notebook.

Exit Criteria:
The child is able to recognize and choose three white items from a magazine.

Lesson R-23

Goal: To Match Colors

Materials:

Box of nine color crayons (red, yellow, blue, black, green, orange, purple, brown and white)
Scissors
Nine markers (red, yellow, blue, black, green, orange, purple, brown and white)
27 colored beads (nine of each color)
Nine colored scraps of paper (red, yellow, blue, black, green, orange, purple, brown and white)
Lesson Illustration

Implementation:

1. Color the pictures of color crayons from Lesson Illustration R-23. Cut the crayon pictures apart.

2. As you lay down each crayon picture, name it and point to the color word.

3. Have the child match each color crayon to its picture.

4. Mix up the other items.

5. One at a time, let the child match the objects to the appropriate color by placing the object next to or under the appropriate crayon picture. As he matches each object to the correct crayon picture, name the color.

6. Continue until all the items have been correctly separated.

Exit Criteria:
    The child is able to match all objects to the appropriate color.

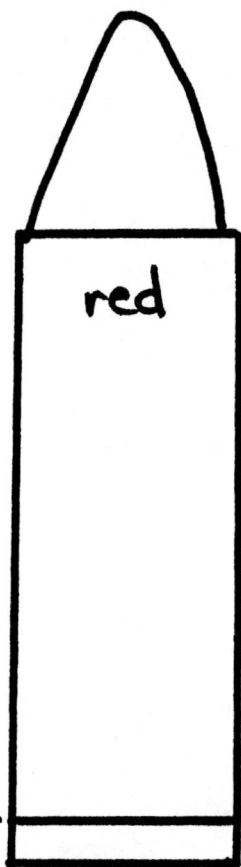 red

 yellow

 blue

 green

 brown

 black

 orange

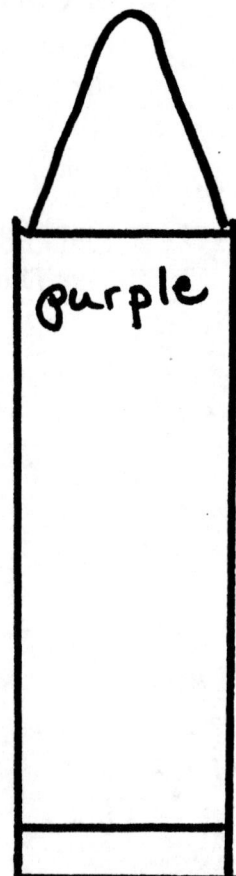 purple

Lesson R-24

Goal: To Match Colors

Materials:
18 index cards (3" × 5")
Nine colored markers (red, yellow, blue, black, green, orange, purple, brown and
    white)
Envelope

Implementation:

1. Color one index card blue. Say the name, "Blue."

2. Repeat with each color until all nine colors have been used.

3. Let the child color nine index cards, one color per card.

4. Mix all the cards together and lay them face down on a table or other flat surface.

5. Play "Concentration" with the child. Name each color as it is turned up. Play
   until all the cards have been matched.

6. Put the cards in an envelope and store the envelope in the notebook for later
   use.

   Exit Criteria:
       The child is able to match each color card to its mate.

Lesson R-25

Goal: To Match Colors to Objects in the Environment

Materials:

Nine pieces of colored paper (red, yellow, blue, black, green, orange, purple, brown and white)

Implementation:

1. With all nine pieces of colored paper in hand, take the child for a walk around the room, school or neighborhood.
2. Have the child find things that match the color of the pieces of paper in his environment.
3. Continue until the child finds at least two items in each color. Name each item as he finds it. (For example, "That is a green bush." "That is a red stop sign.")
4. If time permits, when you return to the classroom draw a picture of one or two items he found in each color, naming each item as you draw it and labeling each picture.

Exit Criteria:

The child is able to find at least one item in his environment that matches each piece of paper (a total of nine items).

Lesson R-26

Goal: To Separate Items as Big or Small

Materials:

Lesson Illustration
Notebook
Loose leaf paper
Scissors
Paste/glue
Pencil
Envelope

Implementation:

1. Before the lesson, cut apart the BIG and SMALL pictures from the Lesson Illustration. (You need not use all sixteen pairs of pictures in one lesson. You will need at least five or six pairs.)

2. Point to your hands and say, "My hands are big." The point to the child's hands and say, "Your hands are small."

3. Trace the outline of your hand on a piece of paper and label it, "A BIG hand."

4. Trace the outline of the child's hand on a piece of paper and label it, "A SMALL hand."

5. Point to other things that are big in the room or in magazines. Try to find their small counterparts. Name them.

6. Label one piece of paper "BIG" and one piece, "SMALL."

7. Get the pairs of pictures from the Lesson Illustration. Put one big item on the BIG page and one small item on the SMALL page. Name each item and state its size as you put it on the appropriate page. (For example, "This is a big fish. I will put it on the BIG page.")

8. Repeat for at least three objects.

9. Let the child match the next objects to the correct page. Name the item and state its size as he matches them.

10. Continue until the child matches three items correctly and independently.

11. Put the pairs of pictures in an envelope and store the envelope in the child's notebook for later use.

Exit Criteria:
   The child must correctly place three sets of pictures on the BIG and SMALL pages.

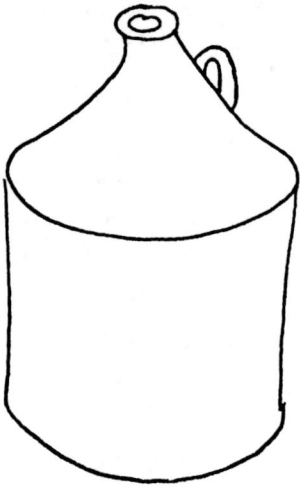

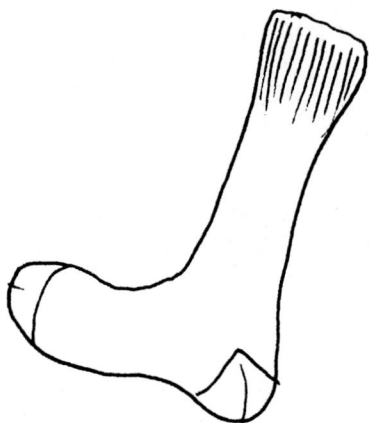

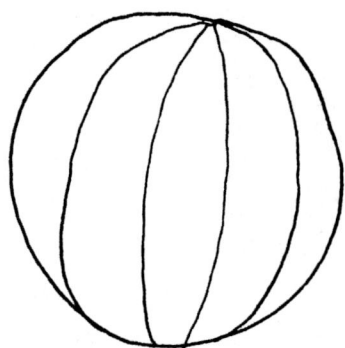

78

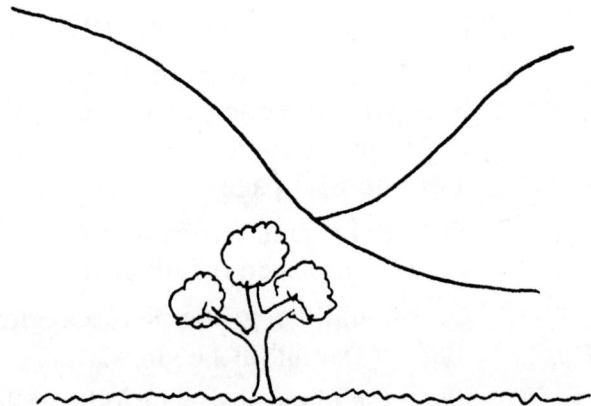

Lesson R-27

Goal: To Separate Items as Big or Small

Materials:

One set of pairs of pictures from Lesson R-26
Notebook
Loose leaf paper
Scissors
Paste/glue
Pencil

Implementation:

1. Point to your hands and say, "My hands are big." Then point to the child's hands and say, "Your hands are small."

2. Trace the outline of your hand on a piece of paper and label it, "A BIG hand."

3. Trace the outline of the child's hand on a piece of paper and label it, "A SMALL hand."

4. Point to other things that are big in the room or in a magazine. Try to find their small counterparts. Name each object you find.

5. Label one piece of paper "BIG" and one piece of paper "SMALL."

6. Get the pairs of pictures from Lesson Illustration R-26. Put one big item on the BIG page and one small item on the SMALL page. Name each item and its size as you put it on the appropriate page. (For example, "This is a big fish. I will put it on the BIG page.")

7. Follow the same procedure for the other pairs of pictures until all the pictures have been placed on either the BIG or SMALL page.

8. Let the child glue the pictures onto the appropriate page. Name them as either "big" or "small" as he glues.

9. Place the glued sheets into the child's notebook.

Exit Criteria:
   The child must correctly place 10 of the 16 items on the appropriate page.

Lesson R-28

Goal: To Match Shapes: ROUND

Materials:

Lesson Illustration
Loose leaf paper
Notebook
Pencils
Color crayons
Scissors
Paste/glue
Magazines
Ball

Implementation:

1. Label a piece of paper, "ROUND." Draw a circle on the ROUND page.
2. Trace the child's finger around the circle, telling him, "It is round."
3. Show the child the ball, saying, "The ball is round." Draw the ball onto the ROUND page.
4. Look through the magazine with the child and find at least three round items.
5. Cut out the magazine pictures you find and paste them onto the ROUND page.
6. Color the circles from the Lesson Illustration. Cut them out and paste them onto the ROUND page.

Exit Criteria:
   The child must be able to find one round item in a magazine.

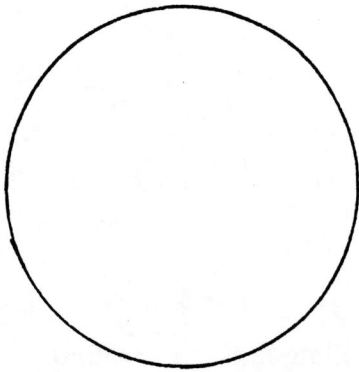 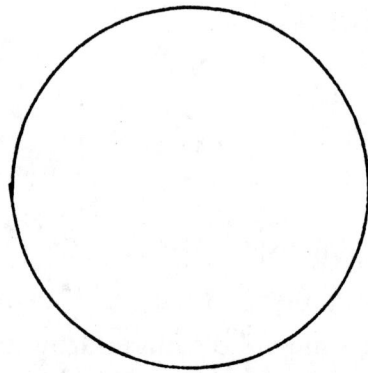

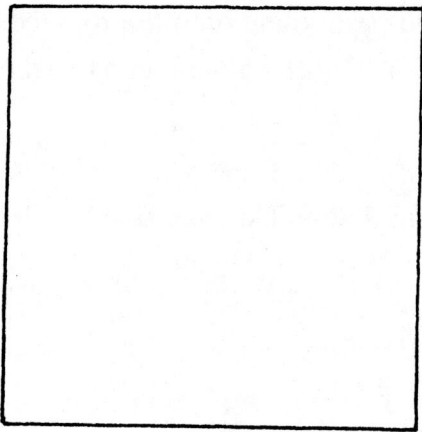 

Lesson R-29

Goal: To Match Shapes: ROUND

Materials:

Magazines
Lesson Illustration
Color crayons
Scissors
Paste/glue
Loose leaf paper

Implementation:

1. Show the child the Lesson Illustration. Have the child trace his finger around the round objects. Tell him, "The balloon is round. The clock is round," etc., as he traces each round object in the picture.

2. Look through magazines together and have the child find round objects. Cut them out and label each one as round.

3. Have the child draw something round. Label it.

4. Paste all the round pictures into the notebook on the ROUND page from Lesson R-28. (If necessary, start a new ROUND page.)

   Exit Criteria:
   The child must identify five round objects in a magazine. (For example, ball, fruit, wheel, tire, candy)

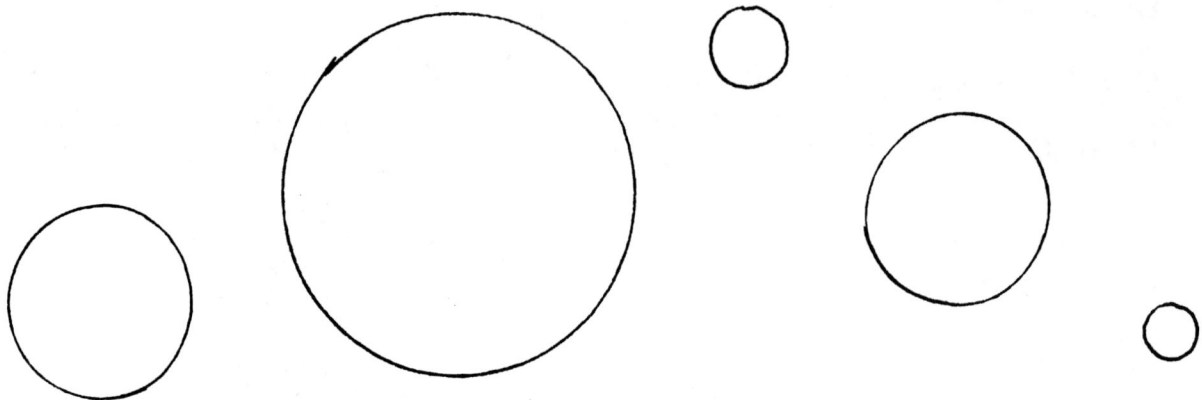

Lesson R-30

Goal: To Match Shapes: SQUARE

Materials:

Lesson Illustration
Loose leaf paper
Pencils
Color crayons
Scissors
Paste/glue
Magazines
Block/square

Implementation:

1. Label a piece of paper, "SQUARE." Draw a square on the SQUARE page.

2. Trace the child's finger around the square, saying, "This is a square."

3. Trace your finger around the square, naming it.

4. Look around the room and see if you can find any square objects. Point them out to the child, naming each one. (For example, "The block is square.")

5. Look through the magazines with the child and find at least three square objects. Cut out the square objects you find and paste them onto the SQUARE page.

6. Color the squares on the Lesson Illustration. Cut them out and paste them onto the SQUARE page.

Exit Criteria:
    The child must identify one square item from a magazine.

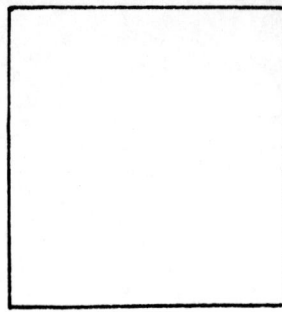

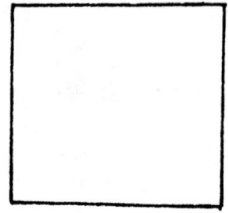

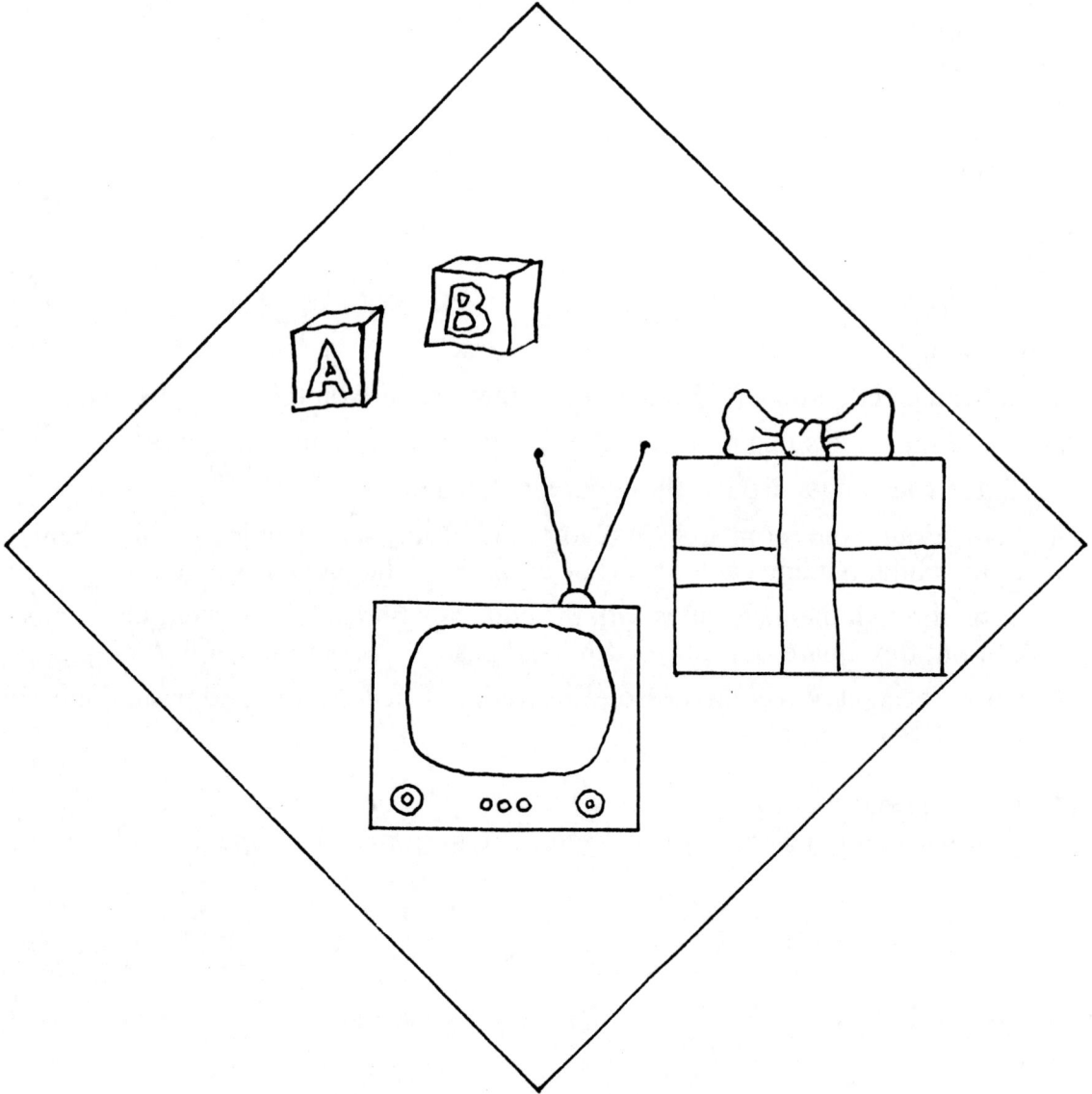

Lesson R-31

Goal: To Discriminate Between Shapes: ROUND/SQUARE

Materials:

Lesson Illustrations R-29 and R-30
Paste/glue
Loose leaf paper
Scissors

Implementation:

1. Label the top of one sheet of paper "SQUARE" and the other, "ROUND."
2. Cut apart the pictures from Lesson Illustrations R-29 and R-30.
3. Name each one as round or square.
4. Let the child choose one and place it on the appropriate page, SQUARE or ROUND.
5. Repeat for all the pictures.
6. Glue each picture onto the appropriate page.
7. Place the SQUARE and ROUND pages in the notebook.

Exit Criteria:
   The child must correctly identify eight of the pictures as round or square.

Lesson R-32

Goal: To Match Shapes: TRIANGLE

Materials:

Lesson Illustration
Loose leaf paper
Pencil
Color crayons
Scissors
Paste/glue
Magazine
Construction paper

Implementation:

1. Label a piece of paper, "TRIANGLE." Draw a triangle on the TRIANGLE page.

2. Trace the child's finger around the triangle, saying, "This is a triangle."

3. Trace your finger around the triangle, naming it.

4. Look around the room and see if you can find any triangular objects. Point them out to the child, naming each one. (For example, "The pennant is a triangle.")

5. Look through the magazine with the child and try to find at least three triangular objects. Cut out the triangular objects you find and past them onto the TRIANGLE page. OR: Cut out a triangle from construction paper and paste it onto the TRIANGLE page. Have the child cut out a triangle and paste it onto the TRIANGLE page.

6. Color the triangles on the Lesson Illustration. Cut them out and paste them onto the TRIANGLE page.

7. Place the TRIANGLE page into the notebook.

Exit Criteria:
The child must identify one triangular item from a magazine or must cut out a triangle.

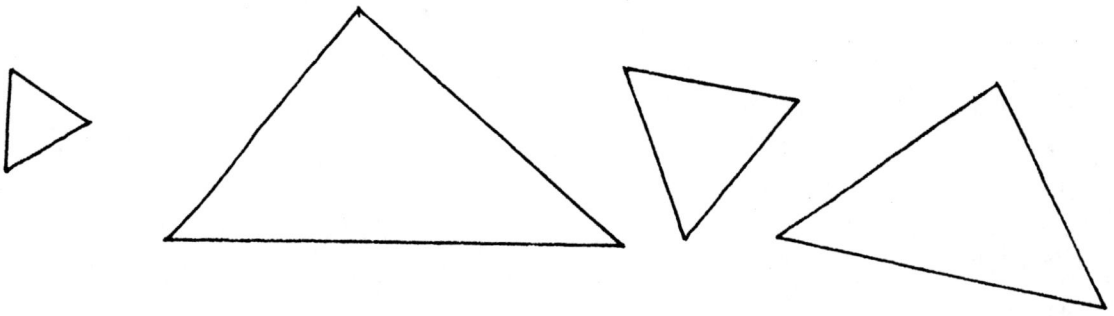

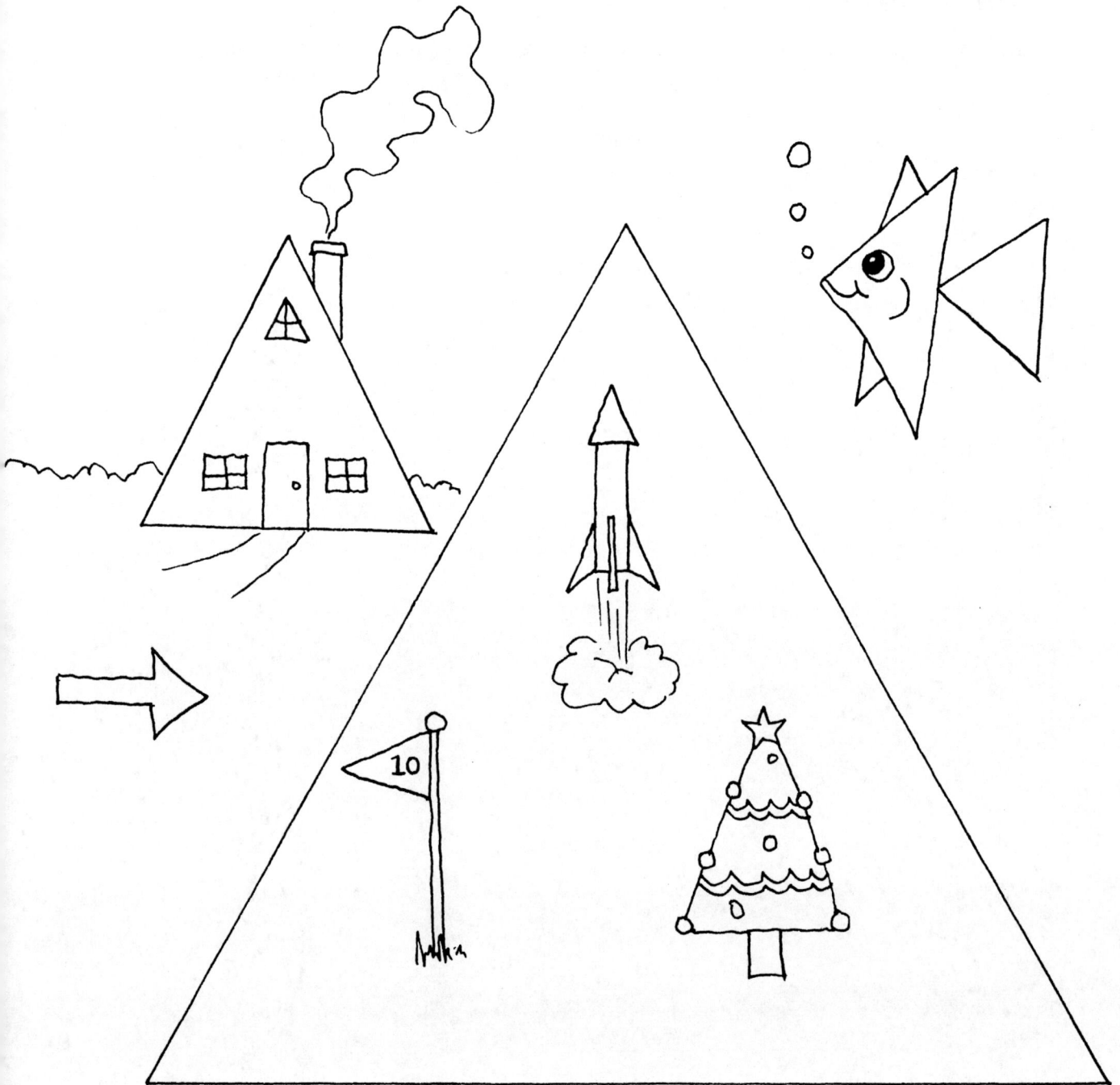

Lesson R-33

Goal: To Work With Shapes

Materials:

Paste/glue
Small and large triangles, squares and circles cut out of construction paper
Loose leaf paper

Implementation:

1. Let the child paste shapes onto a sheet of loose leaf paper. Point out the different objects he can make, such as a house from a triangle and a square:

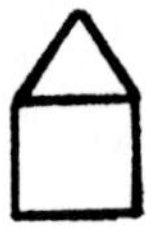

   Label each shape as he pastes it onto the sheet.
2. Place the sheet in the notebook.

   Exit Criteria:
        The child must paste shapes onto the page.

Lesson R-34

Goal: To Recognize Prepositions: UNDER

Materials:

Lesson Illustration
Ball
Index card
Crayon
Scissors
Envelope

Implementation:

1. Take the ball and place it under a table.

2. Write or print "UNDER" on the index card. Show the card to the child and say, "The ball is *under* the table."

3. Place the ball under a chair. Show the UNDER card to the child. Let the child place the ball under a table or chair.

4. Cut apart the items in the Lesson Illustration.

5. Lay the picture of the workbench on a flat surface. Have the child place each item under the workbench in the picture when you show him the word UNDER.

6. Place the workbench picture and other items in the envelope and store the envelope in the child's notebook for later use.

   Exit Criteria:
   The child must be able to place the items under the workbench when shown the word UNDER.

HAMMER

SCREWDRIVER

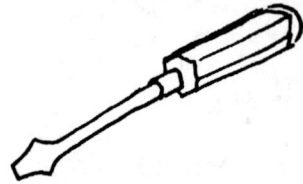

PUT THE TOOLS
UNDER THE WORKBENCH

SAW

PLIERS

LADDER

Lesson R-35

Goal: To Recognize Prepositions: ON

Materials:

Lesson Illustration
Ball
Index card
Crayon
Scissors
Envelope

Implementation:

1. Take the ball and place it on a table.
2. Write or print "ON" on the index card. Show the card to the child and say, "The ball is *on* the table."
3. Place the ball on a chair. Show the ON card to the child. Let the child place the ball on the table or chair.
4. Cut apart the items in the Lesson Illustration.
5. Lay the picture of the table on a flat surface. Have the child place each item on the table in the picture when you show him the word ON.
6. Place the table picture and other items in the envelope and store the envelope in the notebook for late use.

Exit Criteria:
     The child must be able to place the items on the table when shown the word ON.

HAMBURGER  MILK  APPLES  CAKE

PUT THE FOOD
ON THE TABLE

BREAD 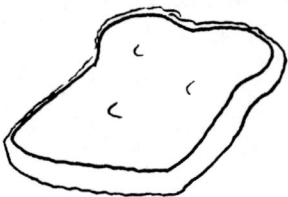 CHEESE  EGGS  SODA

Lesson R-36

Goal: To Recognize Prepositions: IN

Materials:

Lesson Illustration
Ball
Index card
Crayon
Scissors
Envelope
Box
Basket

Implementation:

1. Take the ball and place it in a box.
2. Write or print "IN" on the index card. Show the card to the child and say, "The ball is *in* the box."
3. Place the ball in a basket. Show the IN card to the child. Let the child place the ball in a box or basket.
4. Cut apart the items in the Lesson Illustration.
5. Lay the picture of the basket on a flat surface. Have the child place each item in the basket in the picture when you show him the word IN.
6. Place the picture of the basket and the other items in the envelope and store the envelope in the notebook for later use.

Exit Criteria:

The child must be able to place the items in the basket when shown the word IN.

PUT THE TOYS
IN THE BASKET

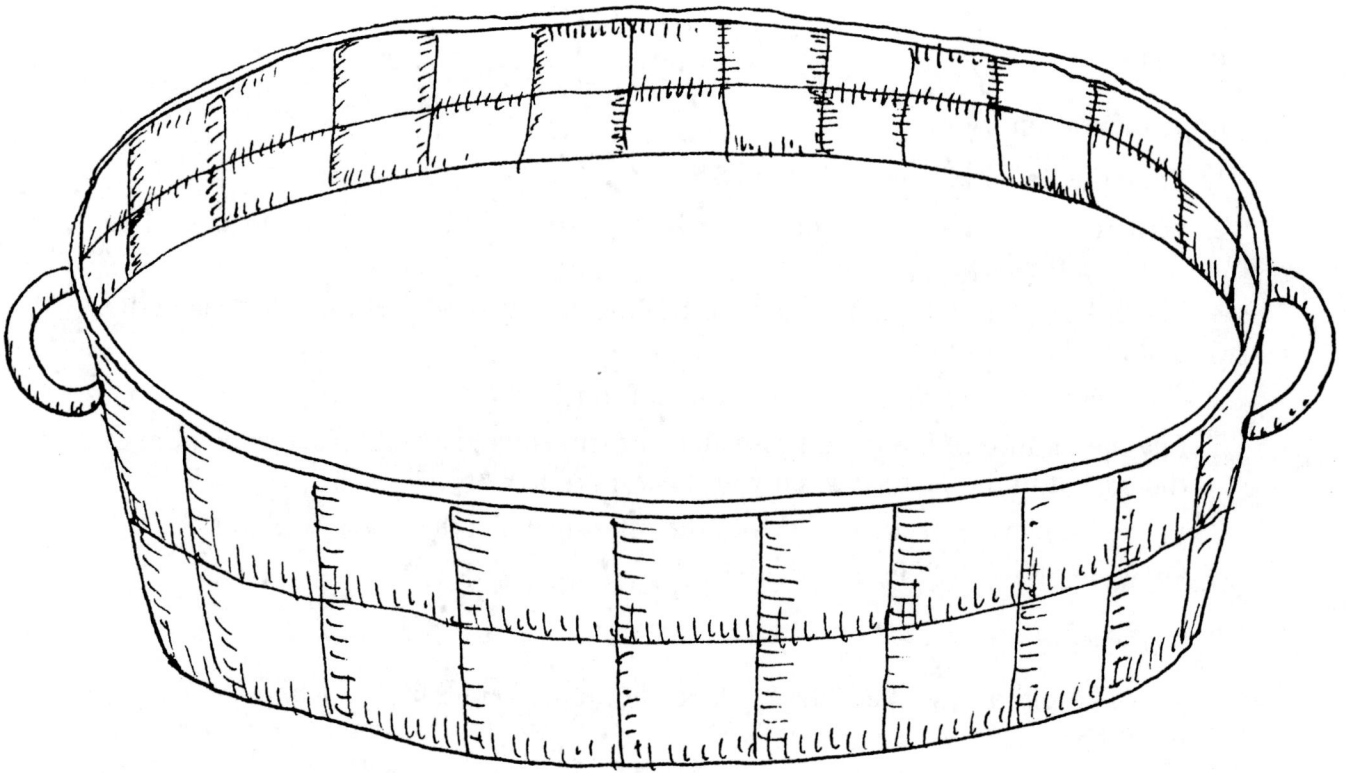

JUMP ROPE

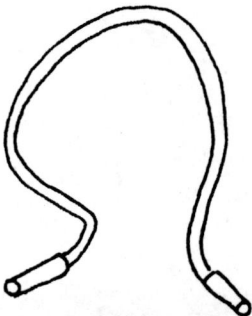

BALL

DOLL

Lesson R-37

Goal: To Discriminate Between Prepositions: IN, ON, UNDER

Materials:

Ball
Two other toys
ON index card
IN index card
UNDER index card

Implementation:

1. Mix up the index cards. Lay them face down.

2. Give the child the ball. Let the child choose one of the index cards.

3. The child must follow the instruction on the card he chooses. (For example, if he chooses the UNDER card, he is to put the ball under an object in the room.) Help him if he needs it.

4. Repeat for all three cards with each of the three toys.

5. Take a turn picking cards and placing the toys for all three prepositions and all three toys.

Exit Criteria:
   The child must be able to correctly place six items according to the prepositions.

Lesson R-38

Goal: To Discriminate Between Prepositions: IN, ON, UNDER

Materials:

Envelopes from Lessons R-34—R-36.
Paste/glue
Loose leaf paper
IN index card
ON index card
UNDER index card

Implementation:

1. Take out the pictures of the workbench, table and basket. Lay them on a flat surface. Take out all the other pictures of the smaller items.
2. Hand the child the first item. Show him one preposition index card and help him put the item on the correct page. (That is, *under* the workbench, *on* the table, or *in* the basket)
3. Continue to have the child place the items in the appropriate positions. Alternate presentation of the prepositions.
4. After the child has placed all the items in the appropriate positions on the appropriate pictures, glue the items onto each picture. Label the pictures "ON", "IN" or "UNDER."
5. Glue each picture onto a sheet of loose leaf paper and place the sheets in the notebook.

Exit Criteria:
    The child must be able to place each item correctly on the appropriate picture.

Lesson R-39

Goal: To Review Prepositions: IN, ON, UNDER

Materials:

Lesson Illustration
Scissors
Crayon
Loose leaf paper
Paste/glue
IN index card
ON index card
UNDER index card

Implementation:

1. Cut the pictures apart.
2. Have the child find pairs and match them with the appropriate index card. (For example, the hand goes *in* the glove.)
3. Have the child continue for all picture pairs.
4. Label three sheets of paper "IN", "ON" and "UNDER", respectively. Paste each pair onto the appropriate page.
5. Put the pages into the child's notebook.

Exit Criteria:

The child must be able to correctly match each pair of pictures to the appropriate preposition.

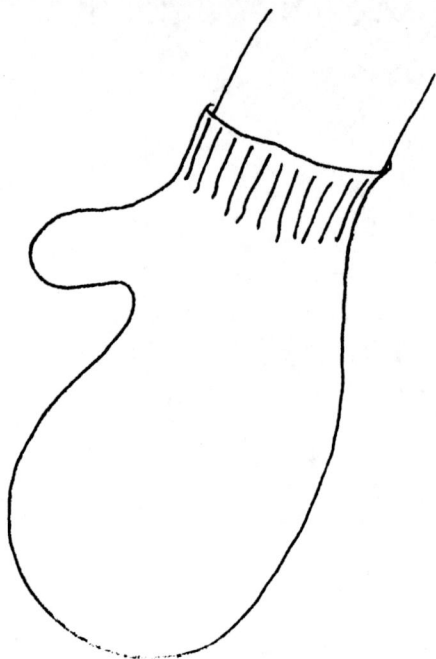

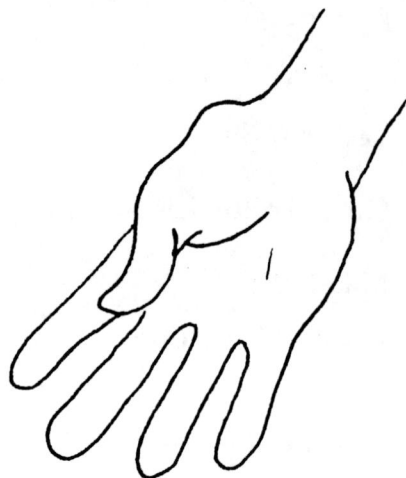

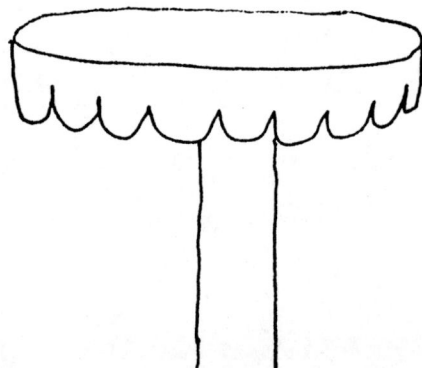

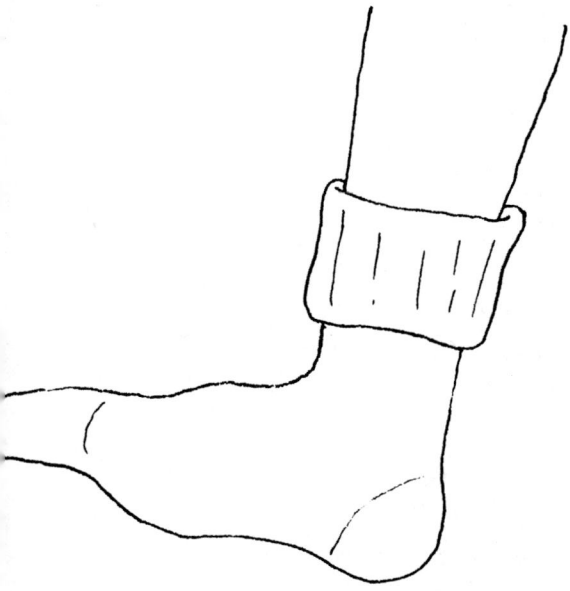
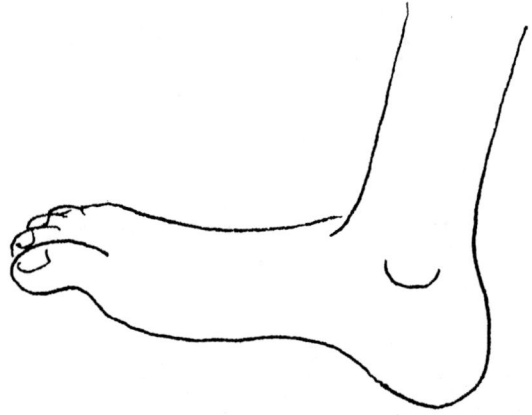

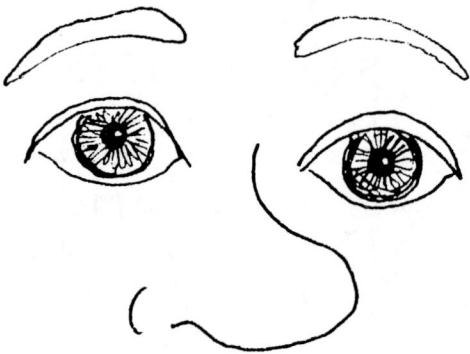
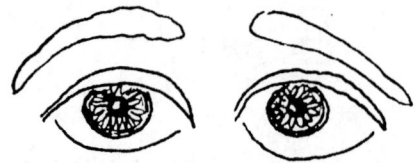

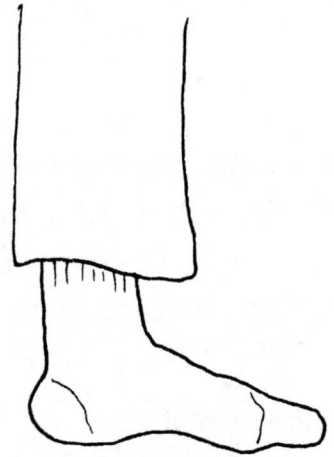

Lesson R-40

Goal: To Sequence Daily Activities: CHILD

Materials:

Lesson Illustration
Scissors
Index cards
Paste/glue
Envelope

Implementation:

1. Cut apart the pictures in the Lesson Illustration. Have the child look at all the pictures with you.
2. Point to the picture which depicts the first event of the child's day. Name it. (For example, "I wake up." or "waking up")
3. Have the child choose the picture which comes next in the sequence of his daily activities. Name it. (For example, "I eat breakfast." or "eating breakfast")
4. Continue until all the pictures have been chosen.
5. Mix up the pictures and have the child put them into the proper sequence.
6. Paste each picture onto an index card.
7. Place the cards in an envelope and put the envelope in the notebook for later use.

Exit Criteria:
   The child must be able to place the pictures in the correct order.

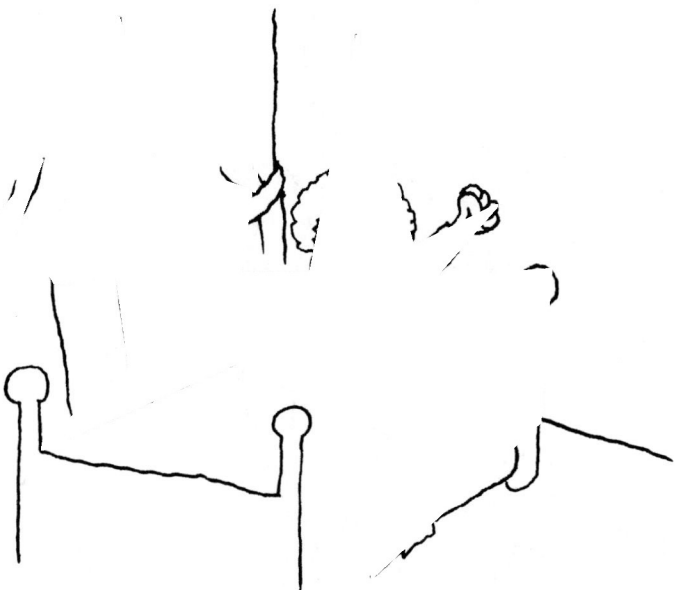

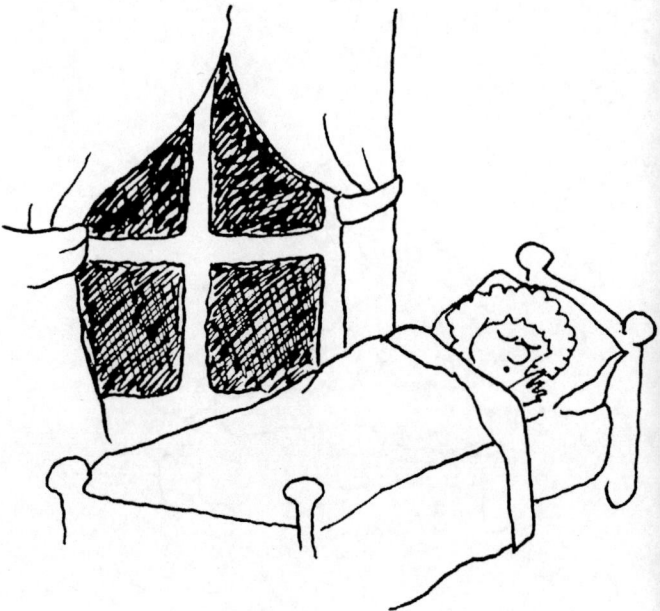

Lesson R-41

Goal: To Sequence Daily Activities: MOTHER

Materials:

Lesson Illustration
Scissors
Index cards
Paste/glue
Envelope

Implementation:

1. Cut apart the pictures in the Lesson Illustration. Have the child look at all the pictures with you.

2. Pick out the picture which depicts the first event in Mother's day. Name it. (For example, "Mother gets up." or "getting up")

3. Have the child choose the picture which comes next in the sequence of Mother's daily activities. Name it. (For example, "Mother brushes her hair." or "brushing hair")

4. Continue until the child has chosen all the pictures that depict his mother's day. (Note: Not all of the pictures may be applicable. Let the child tell you what his mother does. For instance, some mothers may go to work, some may not. Some mothers may sew, some may not.)

5. Mix up all the pictures the child has chosen and have the child put them into the proper sequence.

6. Paste each picture the child has chosen onto an index card.

7. Place the cards in an envelope and put the envelope in the notebook for later use.

Exit Criteria:
    The child must be able to place the pictures in the correct order.

Lesson R-42

Goal: To Sequence Daily Activities: FATHER

Materials:

Lesson Illustration
Scissors
Index cards
Paste/glue
Envelope

Implementation:

1. Cut apart the pictures in the Lesson Illustration. Have the child look at all the pictures with you.

2. Pick out the picture which depicts the first event in Father's day. Name it. (For example, "Father wakes up" or "waking up")

3. Have the child choose the picture which comes next in the sequence of Father's day. Name it. (For example, "Father brushes his teeth" or "brushing teeth")

4. Continue until the child has chosen all the pictures which depict his father's day. (Note: Not all the pictures may be applicable. Let the child tell you what his father does. For instance, some fathers may go to work, some may not. Some fathers may cook breakfast, some may not.)

5. Mix up the pictures the child has chosen and have the child put them into the proper sequence.

6. Paste each picture the child has chosen onto an index card.

7. Place the cards in an envelope and put the envelope in the notebook for later use.

Exit Criteria:
    The child must be able to place the pictures in the correct order.

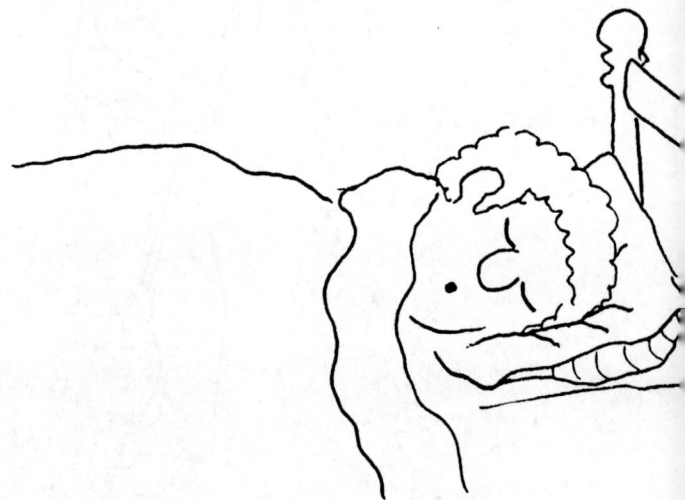

Lesson R-43

Goal: To Recognize Activities the Child Likes

Materials:

Magazines
Paste/glue
Scissors
Loose leaf paper

Implementation:

1. Look through magazines and have the child choose pictures of what he likes to do.
2. Cut out the pictures and paste each one on a separate piece of paper. Label each page.
3. Continue until you have at least five activities.
4. Place the pages in the notebook.

Exit Criteria:
The child must be able to choose at least five activities.

Lesson R-44

Goal: To Recognize Shapes: CIRCLE

Materials:

Lesson Illustration
Color crayons
Loose leaf paper
Circle cut out of construction paper

Implementation:

1. Show the child the construction paper circle and name it.
2. Take a walk around the school and have the child point out objects that are round. Note the items he finds.
3. Back in the classroom, have the child draw some circles or some of the objects he saw on the walk. (If desired, let him use the second Lesson Illustration.)
4. Show the child the Lesson Illustrations and have the child point out and trace circles in the objects pictured.
5. The child may color each object as he finds the circles in it.
6. On the first Lesson Illustration, have the child color one *small* circle and one *big* circle. Label each circle he colors.

Exit Criteria:

The child must be able to identify (or trace on the Lesson Illustrations) at least four items that are round or have a circular shape.

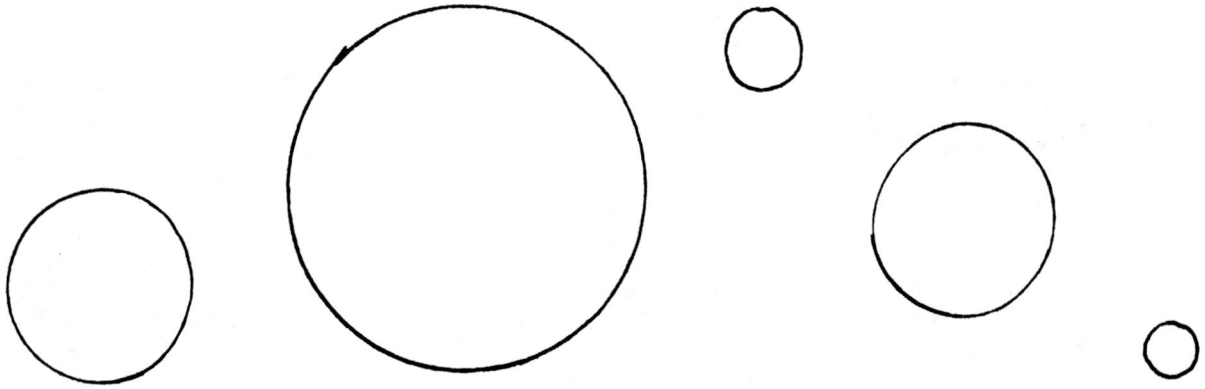

Make something round.

Lesson R-45

Goal: To Recognize Shapes: SQUARE

Materials:

Lesson Illustration
Color crayons
Loose leaf paper
Square cut out of construction paper

Implementation:

1. Show the child the construction paper square and name it.
2. Take a walk around the school and have the child point out objects that are square. Note the items he finds.
3. Back in the classroom, have the child draw some squares or some of the objects he saw on the walk. (If desired, let him use the second Lesson Illustration.)
4. Show the child the Lesson Illustrations, and have the child point out and trace squares in the objects pictured.
5. The child may color each object as he finds the square in it.
6. On the first Lesson Illustration, have the child color one *small* square and one *big* square. Label each square he colors.

Exit Criteria:
   The child must be able to identify (or trace on the Lesson Illustrations) at least four items that are square.

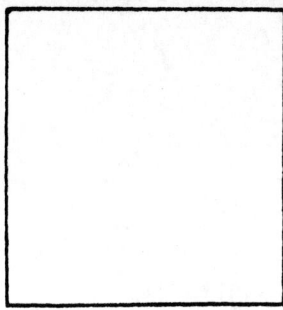

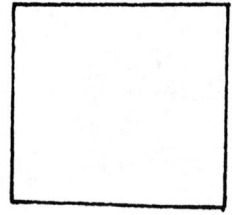

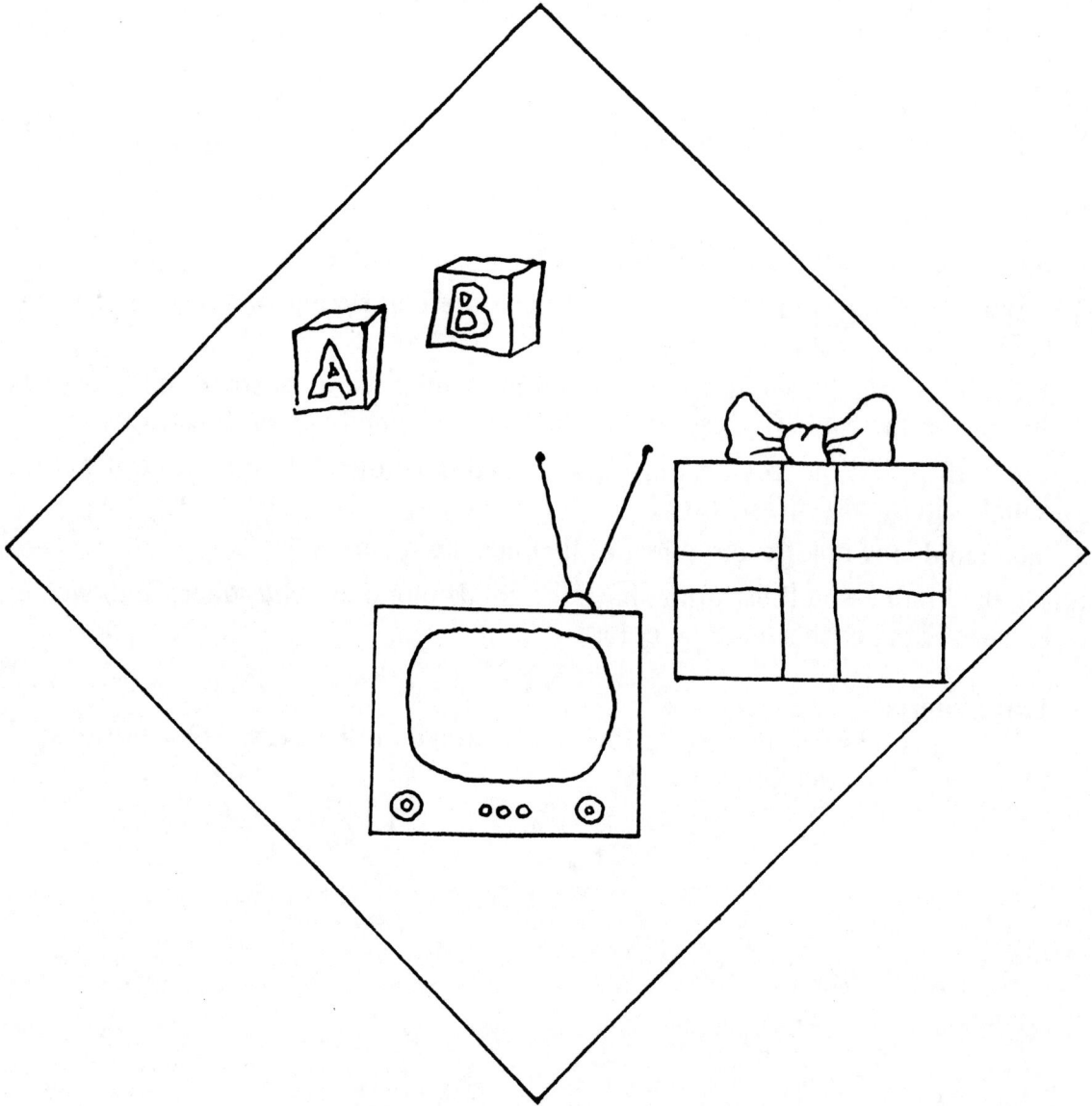

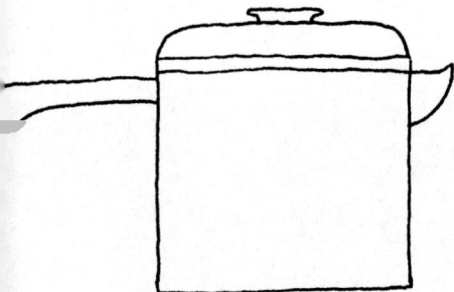

Make something from a square.

119

Lesson R-46

Goal: To Recognize Shapes: TRIANGLE

Materials:

Lesson Illustration
Color crayons
Loose leaf paper
Triangle cut out of construction paper

Implementation:

1. Show the child the construction paper triangle and name it.

2. Take a walk around the school and have the child point down objects that are triangular. Note the items he finds.

3. Back in the classroom, have the child draw some triangles or some of the objects he saw on the walk.

4. Show the child the Lesson Illustration and have the child point out and trace triangles in the objects pictured.

5. The child may color each object as he finds the triangle in it.

6. On the Lesson Illustration, have the child color one *small* triangle and one *big* triangle. Label each triangle he colors.

Exit Criteria:
     The child must be able to identify (or trace on the Lesson Illustration) at least four items that are triangular.

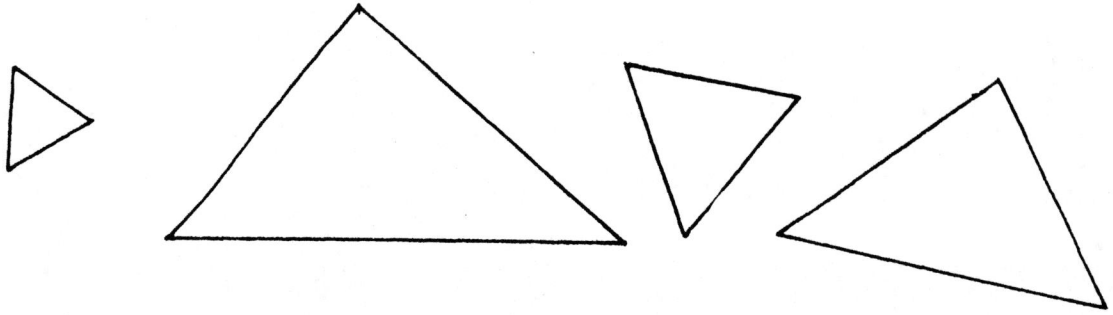

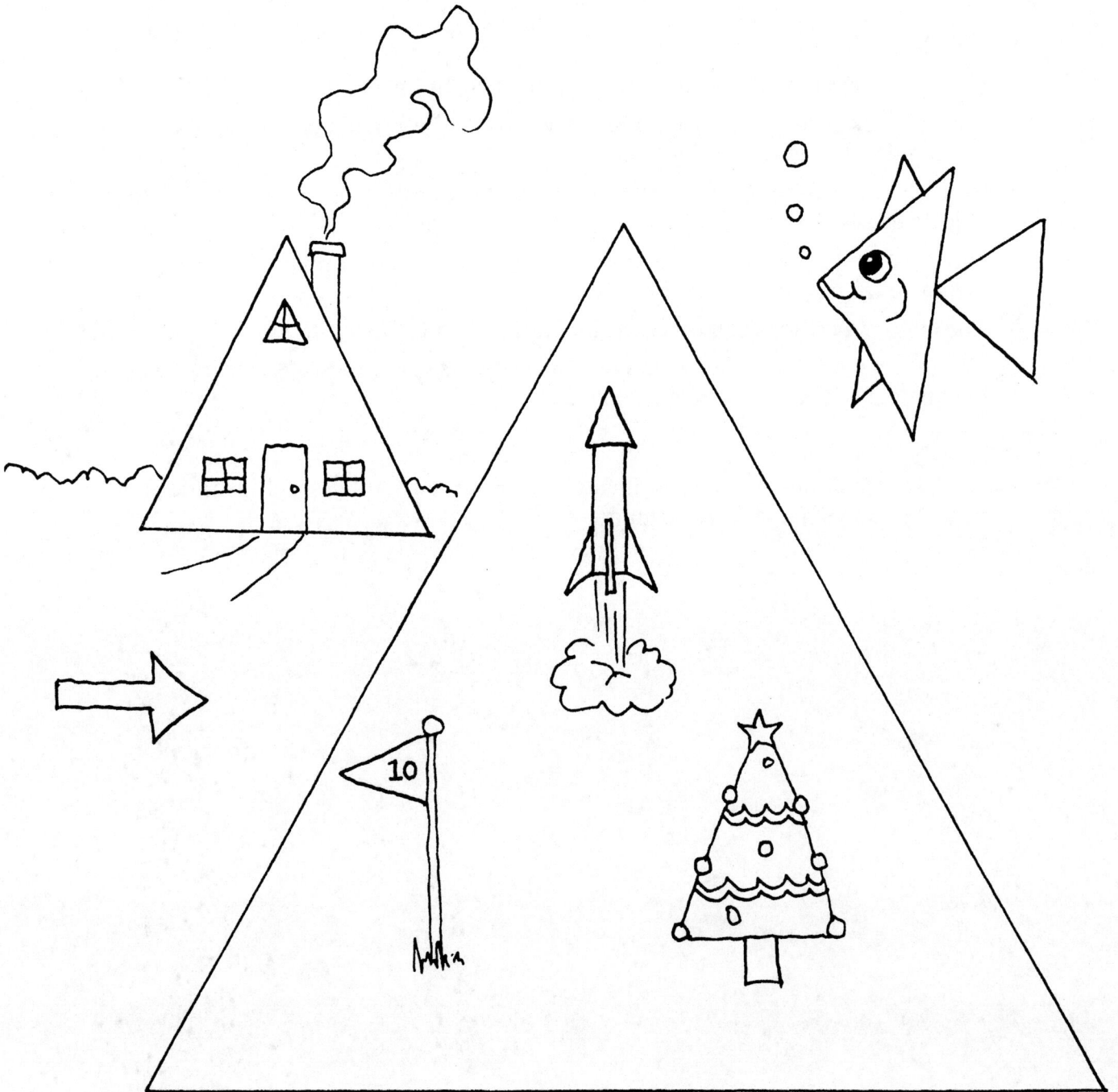

Lesson R-47

Goal: To Recognize Shapes: RECTANGLE

Materials:

Lesson Illustration
Color crayons
Loose leaf paper
Rectangle cut out of construction paper

Implementation:

1. Show the child the construction paper rectangle and name it.
2. Take a walk around the school and have the child point out objects that are rectangular. Note the items he finds.
3. Back in the classroom, have the child draw some rectangles or some of the objects he saw on the walk.
4. Show the child the Lesson Illustration and have the child point out and trace rectangles in the objects pictured.
5. The child may color each object as he finds the rectangle in it.
6. On the Lesson Illustration, have the child color one *small* rectangle and one *big* rectangle. Label each rectangle he colors.

Exit Criteria:
    The child must be able to identify (or trace on the Lesson Illustration) at least four items that are rectangular.

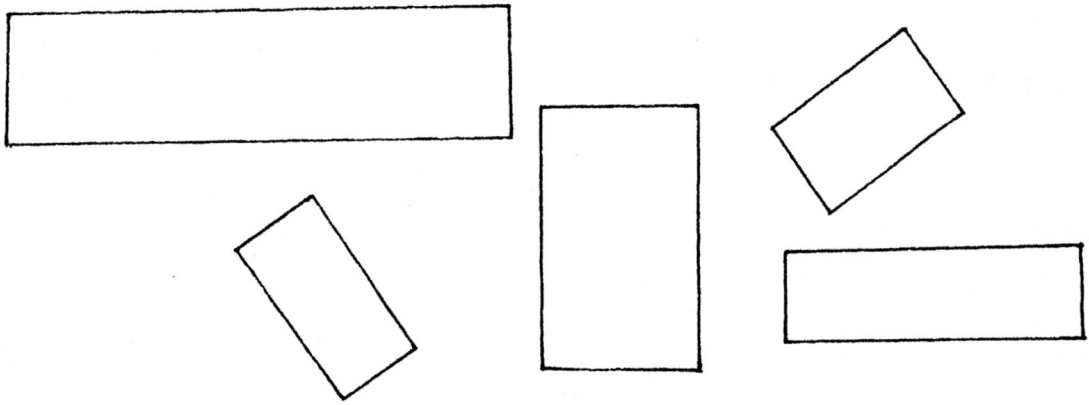

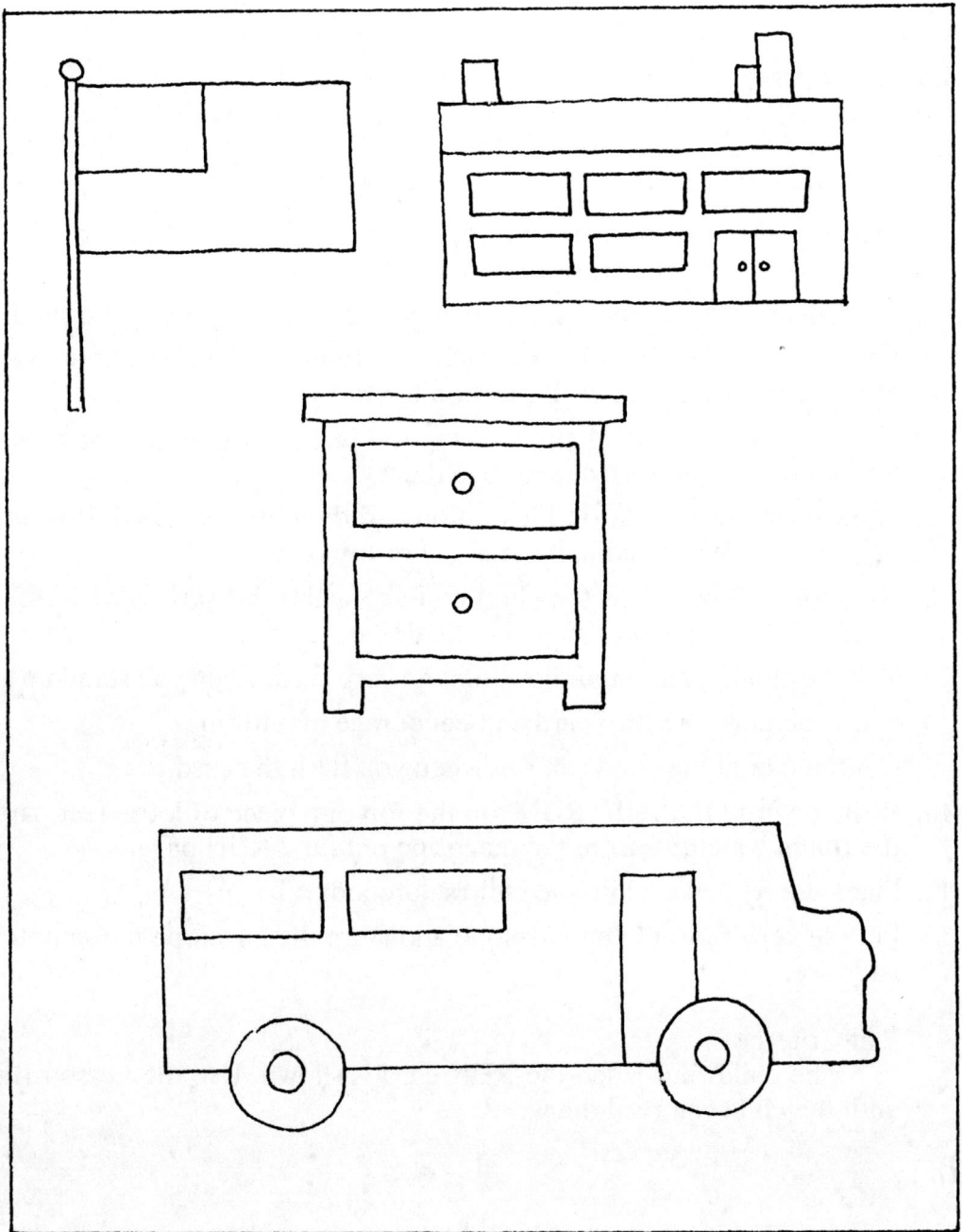

Lesson R-48

Goal: To Recognize Verbs: RUN

Materials:

Lesson Illustration
Index card
Envelope
Marker
Magazine
Scissors
Paste/glue
Loose leaf paper
Toy animal/doll

Implementation:

1. Make a verb card by writing or printing "RUN" on an index card. (Or use a commercially manufactured verb card if available.)
2. Look through a magazine and find a picture of a child, adult or animal running.
3. Let the child find one. As you each find running pictures, show the child the verb card and the Lesson Illustration for RUN.
4. Cut out the magazine pictures. Place the pictures on a table or other flat surface and place the verb card above them.
5. Show the child the Lesson Illustration and then the verb card. Pick up the doll or toy. Say, "Run," and make the doll or toy run.
6. Give the doll or toy to the child and show him the verb card RUN. Tell the child, "Run," and help him make the doll or toy run.
7. Tell the child, "Run," and show him the verb card. Then you stand up and run.
8. Show the child the verb card and encourage him to run.
9. Continue until the child can run when you flash the card.
10. Write or print the verb "RUN" on the top of a piece of loose leaf paper. Paste the running pictures from the magazine onto the RUN page.
11. Place the RUN page into the child's notebook.
12. Put the verb card into an envelope and store the envelope in the notebook for later use.

Exit Criteria:
The child runs when the RUN card is shown. Use the Lesson Illustration until the child can read the word.

JUMP

SITTING

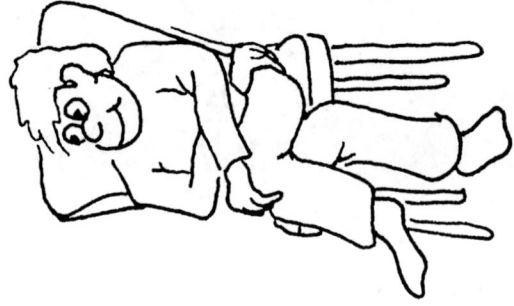

STANDING

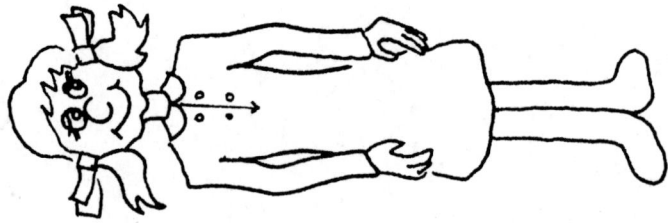

RUN

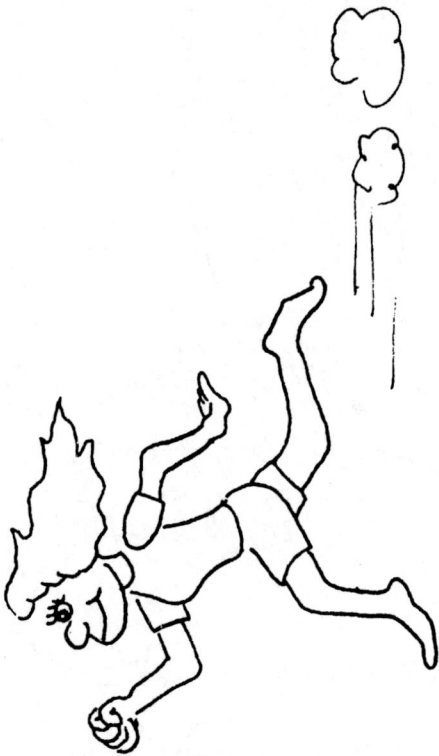

WALK

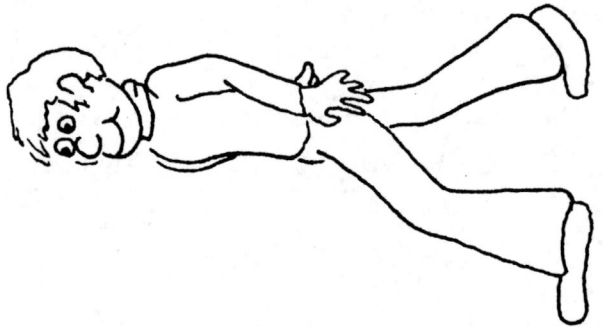

Lesson R-49

Goal: To Recognize Verbs: JUMP

Materials:

Lesson Illustration R-48
Index card
Envelope
Marker
Magazine
Scissors
Loose leaf paper
Paste/glue
Toy animal/doll

Implementation:

1. Make a verb card by writing or printing "JUMP" on an index card. (Or use a commercially manufactured verb card, if available.)

2. Look through a magazine and find a picture of a child, adult or animal jumping.

3. Let the child find one. As you each find jumping pictures, show the child the verb card and the Lesson Illustration for JUMP.

4. Cut out the magazine pictures. Place the pictures on a table or other flat surface and place the verb card above them.

5. Show the child the Lesson Illustration and then the verb card. Pick up the doll or toy. Say, "Jump," and make the doll or toy jump.

6. Give the doll or toy to the child and show him the verb card JUMP. Tell the child, "Jump," and help him make the doll or toy jump.

7. Tell the child, "Jump," and show him the verb card. Then you stand up and jump.

8. Show the child the verb card and encourage him to jump.

9. Continue until the child can jump when you flash the card.

10. Write or print the verb "JUMP" on the top of a piece of loose leaf paper. Paste the jumping pictures from the magazine onto the JUMP page.

11. Mix up the two verb cards (RUN and JUMP) and let the child follow the directions as you flash him each card. When the JUMP card is shown, he jumps. When the RUN card is shown, he runs.

12. Place the JUMP page into the child's notebook.

13. Put the verb card into an envelope and store the envelope in the notebook for later use.

Exit Criteria:
The child jumps when the JUMP card is shown. Use the Lesson Illustration until the child can read the word.

Lesson R-50

Goal: To Recognize Verbs: WALK

Materials:

Lesson Illustration R-48
Index card
Envelope
Marker
Magazine
Scissors
Paste/glue
Loose leaf paper
Toy animal/doll

Implementation:

1. Make a verb card by writing or printing "WALK" on an index card. (Or use a commercially manufactured verb card, if available.)

2. Look through a magazine and find a picture of a child, adult or animal walking.

3. Let the child find one. As you each find walking pictures, show the child the verb card and the Lesson Illustration for WALK.

4. Cut out the magazine pictures. Place the pictures on a table or other flat surface and place the verb card above them.

5. Show the child the Lesson Illustration and then the verb card. Pick up the doll or toy. Say, "Walk," and make the doll or toy walk.

6. Give the doll or toy to the child and show him the verb card WALK. Tell the child, "Walk," and help him make the doll or toy walk.

7. Tell the child, "Walk," and show him the verb card. Then you stand up and walk.

8. Show the child the verb card and encourage him to walk.

9. Continue until the child can walk when you flash the card.

10. Write or print the verb "WALK" on the top of a piece of loose leaf paper. Paste the walking pictures from the magazine onto the WALK page.

11. Mix up all the verb cards (RUN, JUMP and WALK) and let the child follow the directions as you flash him each card. When the RUN card is shown, he runs, etc.

12. Place the WALK page into the child's notebook.

13. Put the verb card into an envelope and store the envelope in the notebook for later use.

Exit Criteria:
   The child walks when the WALK card is shown. Use the Lesson Illustration until the child can read the word.

Lesson R-51

Goal: To Recognize Verbs: STAND UP

Materials:

Lesson Illustration R-48
Index card
Envelope
Marker
Magazine
Scissors
Loose leaf paper
Paste/glue
Toy animal/doll

Implementation:

1. Make a verb card by writing or printing "STAND UP" on an index card. (Or use a commercially manufactured verb card, if available.)
2. Look through a magazine and find a picture of a child, adult or animal standing up.
3. Let the child find one. As you each find standing up pictures, show the child the verb card and the Lesson Illustration for STAND UP.
4. Cut out the magazine pictures. Place the pictures on a table or other flat surface and place the verb card above them.
5. Show the child the Lesson Illustration and then the verb card. Pick up the doll or toy. Say, "Stand up," and make the doll or toy stand up.
6. Give the doll or toy to the child and show him the verb card STAND UP. Tell the child, "Stand up," and help him make the doll or toy stand up.
7. Tell the child, "Stand up," and show him the verb card. Then you stand up.
8. Show the child the verb card and encourage him to stand up.
9. Continue until the child can stand up when you flash the card.
10. Write or print the verb "STAND UP" on the top of a piece of loose leaf paper. Paste the standing up pictures from the magazine onto the STAND UP page.
11. Mix up the verb cards (RUN, JUMP, WALK and STAND UP) and let the child follow the directions as you flash him each card. When the RUN card is shown, he runs, etc.
12. Place the STAND UP page into the child's notebook.
13. Put the verb card into an envelope and store the envelope in the notebook for later use.

Exit Criteria:
    The child stands up when the STAND UP card is shown. Use the Lesson Illustration until the child can read the word.

Lesson R-52

Goal: To Recognize Verbs: SIT DOWN

Materials:

Lesson Illustration R-48
Index card
Envelope
Marker
Magazine
Scissors
Loose leaf paper
Paste/glue
Toy animal/doll

Implementation:

1. Make a verb card by writing or printing "SIT DOWN" on an index card. (Or use a commercially manufactured verb card, if available.)

2. Look through a magazine and find a picture of a child, adult or animal sitting down.

3. Let the child find one. As you each find sitting down pictures, show the child the verb card and the Lesson Illustration for SIT DOWN.

4. Cut out the magazine pictures. Place the pictures on a table or other flat surface and place the verb card above them.

5. Show the child the Lesson Illustration and then the verb card. Pick up the doll or toy. Say, "Sit down," and make the doll or toy sit down.

6. Give the doll or toy to the child and show him the verb card SIT DOWN. Tell the child, "Sit down," and help him make the doll or toy sit down.

7. Tell the child, "Sit down," and show him the verb card. Then you stand up and sit down.

8. Show the child the verb card and encourage him to sit down.

9. Continue until the child can sit down when you flash the card.

10. Write or print the verb "SIT DOWN" on the top of a piece of loose leaf paper. Paste the sitting down pictures from the magazine onto the SIT DOWN page.

11. Mix up the verb cards, (RUN, JUMP, WALK, STAND UP and SIT DOWN) and let the child follow the directions as you flash him each card. When the RUN card is shown, he runs, etc.

12. Place the SIT DOWN page in the child's notebook.

13. Put the verb card in an envelope and store the envelope in the notebook for later use.

Exit Criteria:
    The child sits down when the SIT DOWN card is shown. Use the Lesson Illustration until the child can read the word.

Lesson R-53

Goal: To Recognize Verbs: HOP

Materials:
Lesson Illustration R-48
Index card
Envelope
Marker
Magazine
Scissors
Loose leaf paper
Paste/glue
Toy animal/doll

Implementation:

1. Make a verb card by writing or printing "HOP" on an index card. (Or use a commercially manufactured verb card, if available.)

2. Look through a magazine and find a picture of a child, adult or animal hopping.

3. Let the child find one. As you each find hopping pictures, show the child the verb card and the Lesson Illustration for HOP.

4. Cut out the magazine pictures. Place the pictures on a table or other flat surface and place the verb card above them.

5. Show the child the Lesson Illustration and then the verb card. Pick up the doll or toy. Say, "Hop," and make the doll or toy hop.

6. Give the doll or toy to the child and show him the verb card HOP. Tell the child, "Hop," and help him make the doll or toy hop.

7. Tell the child, "Hop," and show him the verb card. Then you stand up and hop.

8. Show the child the verb card and encourage him to hop.

9. Continue until the child can hop when you flash the card.

10. Write or print the verb "HOP" on the top of a piece of loose leaf paper. Paste the hopping pictures from the magazine onto the HOP page.

11. Mix up the verb cards (RUN, JUMP, WALK, STAND UP, SIT DOWN and HOP) and let the child follow the directions as you flash him each card. When the RUN card is shown, he runs, etc.

12. Place the HOP page in the child's notebook.

13. Put the verb card in an envelope and store the envelope in the notebook for later use.

Exit Criteria:
The child hops when the HOP card is shown. Use the Lesson Illustration until the child can read the word.

Lesson R-54

Goal: To Recognize Verbs: SMILE

Materials:

Lesson Illustration R-48
Index card
Envelope
Marker
Magazine
Scissors
Loose leaf paper
Paste/glue
Toy animal/doll

Implementation:

1. Make a verb card by writing or printing "SMILE" on an index card. (Or use a commercially manufactured verb card, if available.)
2. Look through a magazine and find a picture of a child, adult or animal smiling.
3. Let the child find one. As you each find smiling pictures, show the child the verb card and the Lesson Illustration for SMILE.
4. Cut out the magazine pictures. Place the pictures on a table or other flat surface and place the verb card above them.
5. Show the child the Lesson Illustration and then the verb card. Pick up the doll or toy. Say, "Smile," and make the doll or toy smile.
6. Give the doll or toy to the child and show him the verb card SMILE. Tell the child, "Smile," and help him make the doll or toy smile.
7. Tell the child, "Smile," and show him the verb card. Then you smile.
8. Show the child the verb card and encourage him to smile.
9. Continue until the child can smile when you flash the card.
10. Write or print the verb "SMILE" on the top of a piece of loose leaf paper. Paste the smiling pictures from the magazine onto the SMILE page.
11. Mix up the verb cards (RUN, JUMP, WALK, STAND UP, SIT DOWN, HOP and SMILE) and let the child follow the directions as you flash him each card. When the RUN card is shown, he runs, etc.
12. Place the SMILE page in the child's notebook.
13. Put the verb card in an envelope and store the envelope in the notebook for later use.

   Exit Criteria:
      The child smiles when the SMILE card is shown. Use the Lesson Illustration until the child can read the word.

Lesson R-55

Goal: To Recognize Verbs: MARCH

Materials:

Lesson Illustration R-48
Index card
Envelope
Marker
Magazine
Scissors
Loose leaf paper
Paste/glue
Toy animal/doll

Implementation:

1. Make a verb card by writing or printing "MARCH" on an index card. (Or use a commercially manufactured verb card, if available.)

2. Look through a magazine and find a picture of a child, adult or animal marching.

3. Let the child find one. As you each find marching pictures, show the child the verb card and the Lesson Illustration for MARCH.

4. Cut out the magazine pictures. Place the pictures on a table or other flat surface and place the verb card above them.

5. Show the child the Lesson Illustration and then the verb card. Pick up the doll or toy. Say, "March," and make the doll or toy march.

6. Give the doll or toy to the child and show him the verb card MARCH. Tell the child, "March," and help him make the doll or toy march.

7. Tell the child, "March," and show him the verb card. Then you stand up and march.

8. Show the child the verb card and encourage him to march.

9. Continue until the child can march when you flash the card.

10. Write or print the verb "MARCH" on the top of a piece of loose leaf paper. Paste the marching pictures from the magazine onto the MARCH page.

11. Mix up the verb cards (RUN, JUMP, WALK, STAND UP, SIT DOWN, HOP, SMILE and MARCH) and let the child follow the directions as you flash him each card. When the RUN card is shown, he runs, etc.

12. Place the MARCH page in the child's notebook.

13. Put the verb card in an envelope and store the envelope in the notebook for later use.

Exit Criteria:
   The child marches when the MARCH card is shown. Use the Lesson Illustration until the child can read the word.

Lesson R-56

Goal: To Recognize Verbs: FALL

Materials:

Lesson Illustration R-48
Index card
Envelope
Marker
Magazine
Scissors
Loose leaf paper
Paste/glue
Toy animal/doll

Implementation:

1. Make a verb card by writing or printing "FALL" on an index card. (Or use a commercially manufactured verb card, if available.)

2. Look through a magazine and find a picture of a child, adult or animal falling.

3. Let the child find one. As you each find falling pictures, show the child the verb card and the Lesson Illustration for FALL.

4. Cut out the magazine pictures. Place the pictures on a table or other flat surface and place the verb card above them.

5. Show the child the Lesson Illustration and then the verb card. Pick up the doll or toy. Say, "Fall," and make the doll or toy fall.

6. Give the doll or toy to the child and show him the verb card skip. Tell the child, "Fall," and help him make the doll or toy fall.

7. Tell the child, "Fall," and show him the verb card. Then you stand up and fall.

8. Show the child the verb card and encourage him to fall.

9. Continue until the child falls when you flash the card.

10. Write or print the verb "FALL" on the top of a piece of loose leaf paper. Paste the falling pictures from the magazine onto the FALL page.

11. Mix up the verb cards (RUN, JUMP, WALK, STAND UP, SIT DOWN, HOP, SMILE, MARCH and FALL) and let the child follow the directions as you flash him each card. When the RUN card is shown, he runs, etc.

12. Place the FALL page in the child's notebook.

13. Put the verb card in an envelope and store the envelope in the notebook for later use.

Exit Criteria:
    The child falls when the FALL card is shown. Use the Lesson Illustration until the child can read the word.

Lesson R-57

Goal: To Recognize Verbs: SKIP

Materials:

Lesson Illustration R-48
Index card
Envelope
Marker
Magazine
Scissors
Loose leaf paper
Paste/glue
Toy animal/doll

Implementation:

1. Make a verb card by writing or printing "SKIP" on an index card. (Or use a commercially manufactured verb card, if available.)
2. Look through a magazine and find a picture of a child, adult or animal skipping.
3. Let the child find one. As you each find skipping pictures, show the child the verb card and the Lesson Illustration for SKIP.
4. Cut out the magazine pictures. Place the pictures on a table or other flat surface and place the verb card above them.
5. Show the child the Lesson Illustration and then the verb card. Pick up the doll or toy. Say, "Skip," and make the doll or toy skip.
6. Give the doll or toy to the child and show him the verb card skip. Tell the child, "Skip," and help him make the doll or toy skip.
7. Tell the child, "Skip," and show him the verb card. Then you stand up and skip.
8. Show the child the verb card and encourage him to skip.
9. Continue until the child can skip when you flash the card.
10. Write or print the verb "SKIP" on the top of a piece of loose leaf paper. Paste the skipping pictures from the magazine onto the SKIP page.
11. Mix up the verb cards (RUN, JUMP, WALK, STAND UP, SIT DOWN, HOP, SMILE, MARCH, FALL and SKIP) and let the child follow the directions as you flash him each card. When the RUN card is shown, he runs, etc.
12. Place the SKIP page in the child's notebook.
13. Put the verb card in an envelope and store the envelope in the notebook for later use.

Exit Criteria:
    The child skips when the SKIP card is shown. Use the Lesson Illustration until the child can read the word.

Lesson R-58

Goal: To Recognize Verbs

Materials:

Lesson Illustration R-48
Verb cards from Lessons R-48 through R-57
Paste/glue
Scissors
Index cards

Implementation:

1. Cut apart the pictures in Lesson Illustration R-48. One at a time, have the child match each verb card to its Lesson Illustration. As the child matches them, name each verb for the child and have him call it out after you.

2. Glue each illustration onto an index card.

3. Mix up the verb cards and lay them face down on a table or other flat surface.

4. Mix up the illustrations and lay them face down on a table or other flat surface.

5. Have the child turn over one verb card. Name the verb. Then have the child turn over the illustrations until he finds the matching illustration. When the child turns up the wrong illustration, have him replace it on the table, face down.

6. Continue until the child matches all the verb cards with the correct illustrations.

Exit Criteria:
   The child can match all 10 pairs of verb cards to illustrations.

Lesson R-59

Goal: To Build and Label Rooms in a House

Materials:

Lesson Illustration
Six shoe boxes
Clear plastic wrap
Construction paper
Adhesive tape
Cardboard
Scissors
Paste/glue
Magazines
Stapler
Marker or crayon
Envelope

Implementation:

1. Find a picture of a house in a magazine. Paste it onto a piece of paper and label it, "HOUSE."

2. Show the child the picture and tell him that you are going to build a house.*

3. Staple the six shoe boxes together as shown in Lesson Illustration R-59.

4. Cut out windows and doors.

5. Cover windows with clear plastic wrap. Secure with tape.

6. Find pictures of rooms in magazines. Cut them out and place them in the house. (Do *not* glue them in place.)

7. Make a roof of construction paper and put it on the house.

8. With a marker or crayon, label the following parts of the house:
    Roof
    Floor
    Walls
    Door
    Windows

9. Find magazine pictures of each of the parts of the house listed in Step 8. Cut out and label each picture.

10. Have the child match each picture to the part of the house.

11. Place the magazine pictures of the rooms in an envelope and store the envelope in the notebook for later use.

Exit Criteria:
    The child can match to the corresponding part of the house a picture of the following: Roof   Walls   Windows   Floor   Door

Note: If time is short, you may wish to construct the house (Steps 3-5) in advance of the lesson.

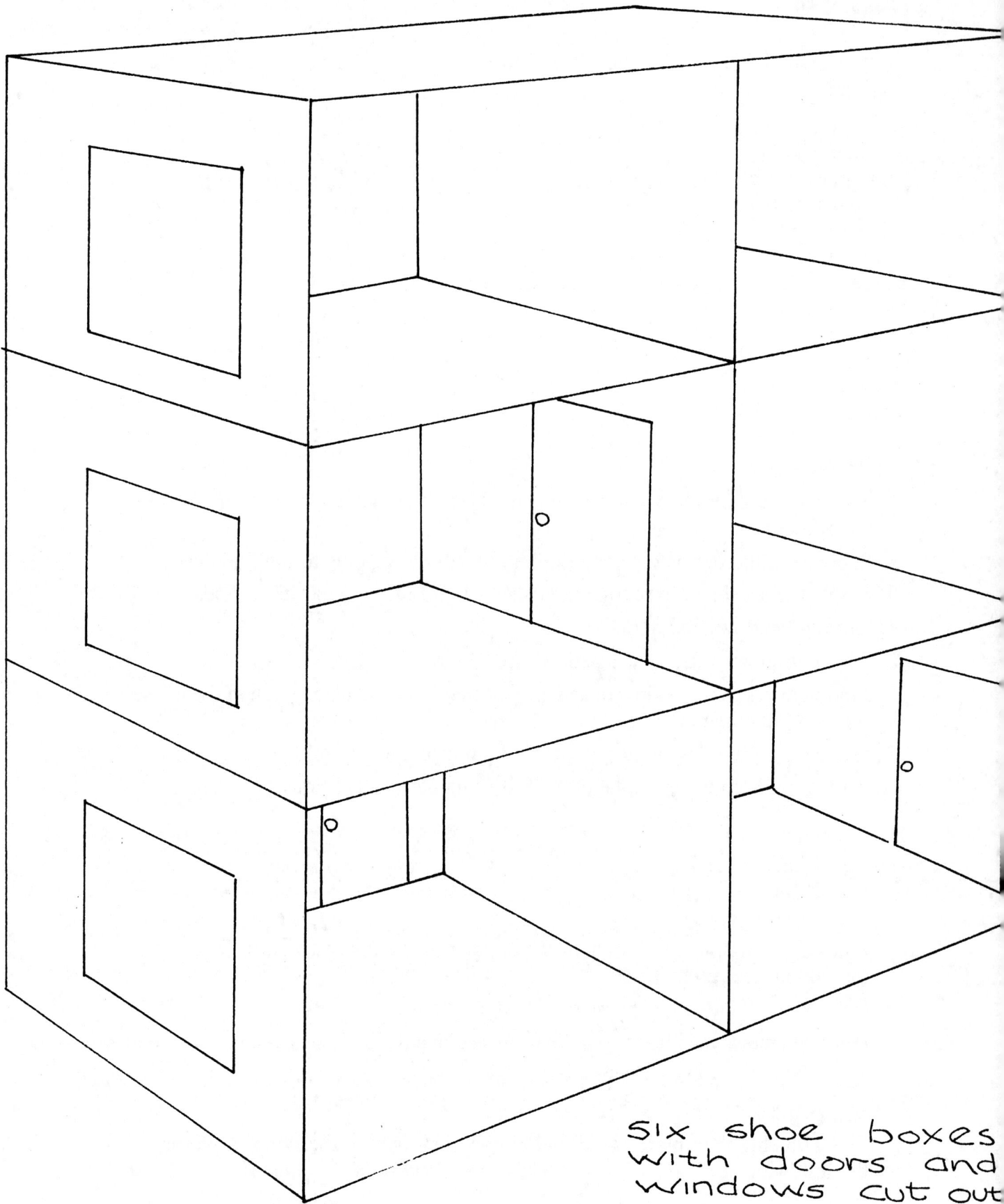

six shoe boxes
with doors and
windows cut out

Lesson R-60

Goal: To Recognize Rooms of a House: KITCHEN

Materials:

Magazines
Lesson Illustration
Scissors
Paste/glue
Construction paper
Fabric
Index cards
Envelope

Implementation:

1. Find a picture of a kitchen in a magazine.

2. Cut out one item in the magazine kitchen and paste it into the house you've made.

3. Have the child find and cut out other kitchen items in the magazine and paste them into the house's kitchen.

4. If you wish, use fabric to make kitchen curtains.

5. Cover the kitchen floor with construction paper if desired.

6. Cut apart the individual pictures in the Lesson Illustration. Mount the pictures individually onto index cards. Label each one.

7. Match the index cards to items pasted in the kitchen.

8. Have the child match the index cards to the items pasted in the kitchen.

9. Place the cards in an envelope and place the envelope in the child's notebook for later use.

   Exit Criteria:
   The child can match all the cards to the kitchen items in the house.

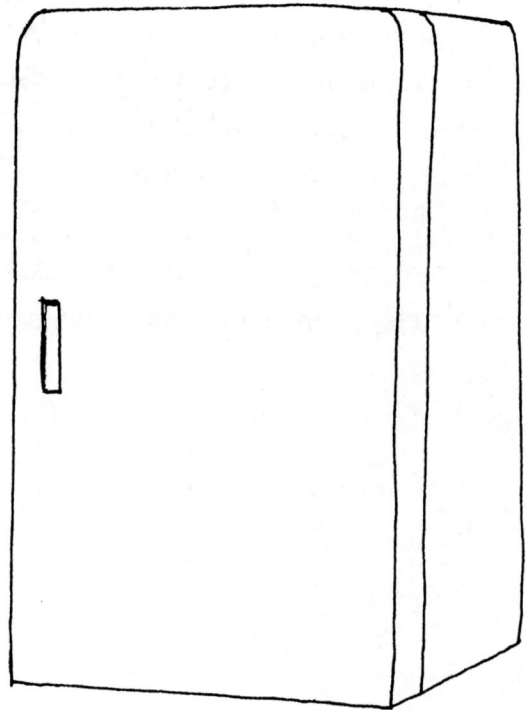

Lesson R-61

Goal: To Recognize Rooms of a House: DINING ROOM

Materials

Magazines
Lesson Illustration
Scissors
Paste/glue
Construction paper
Fabric
Index cards
Envelope

Implementation:

1. Find a picture of a dining room in a magazine.
2. Cut out one item in the magazine dining room and paste it into the house you've made.
3. Have the child find and cut out other dining room items in the magazine and paste them into the house's dining room.
4. If you wish, use fabric to make dining room curtains.
5. Cover the dining room floor with construction paper if desired.
6. Cut apart the individual pictures inthe Lesson Illustration. Mount the pictures individually onto index cards. Label each one.
7. Match the index cards to items pasted in the dining room.
8. Have the child match the index cards to the items pasted in the dining room.
9. Place the cards in an envelope and place the envelope in the child's notebook for later use.

Exit Criteria:
   The child can match all the cards to the dining room items in the house.

Lesson R-62

Goal: To Recognize Rooms of a House: LIVING ROOM

Materials:

Magazines
Lesson Illustration
Scissors
Paste/glue
Construction paper
Fabric
Index cards
Envelope

Implementation:

1. Find a picture of a living room in a magazine.
2. Cut out one item in the magazine living room and paste it into the house you've made.
3. Have the child find and cut out other living room items in the magazine and paste them into the house's living room.
4. If you wish, use fabric to make living room curtains.
5. Cover the living room floor with construction paper if desired.
6. Cut apart the individual pictures in the Lesson Illustration. Mount the pictures individually onto index cards. Label each one.
7. Match the index cards to items pasted in the living room.
8. Have the child match the index cards to the items pasted in the living room.
9. Place the cards in an envelope and place the envelope in the child's notebook for later use.

Exit Criteria:
The child can match all the cards to the living room items in the house.

144

Lesson R-63

Goal: To Recognize Rooms of a House: PARENTS' BEDROOM

Materials:

Magazines
Lesson Illustration
Scissors
Paste/glue
Construction paper
Fabric
Index cards
Envelope

Implementation:

1. Find a picture of an adult's bedroom in a magazine.
2. Cut out one item in the magazine bedroom and paste it into the house you've made.
3. Have the child find and cut out other bedroom items in the magazine and paste them into the house's bedroom.
4. If you wish, use fabric to make bedroom curtains.
5. Cover the bedroom floor with construction paper if desired.
6. Cut apart the individual pictures in the Lesson Illustration. Mount the pictures individually onto index cards. Label each one.
7. Match the index cards to items pasted in the bedroom.
8. Have the child match the index cards to the items pasted in the bedroom.
9. Place the cards in an envelope and place the envelope in the child's notebook for later use.

Exit Criteria:
    The child can match all the cards to the bedroom items in the house.

Lesson R-64

Goal: To Recognize Rooms of a House: CHILD'S BEDROOM

Materials:

Magazines
Lesson Illustration
Scissors
Paste/glue
Construction paper
Fabric
Index cards
Envelope

Implementation:

1. Find a picture of a child's bedroom in a magazine.

2. Cut out one item in the magazine bedroom and paste it into the house you've made.

3. Have the child find and cut out other bedroom items in the magazine and paste them into the house's bedroom.

4. If you wish, use fabric to make bedroom curtains.

5. Cover the bedroom floor with construction paper if desired.

6. Cut apart the individual pictures in the Lesson Illustration. Mount the pictures individually onto index cards. Label each one.

7. Match the index cards to items pasted in the bedroom.

8. Have the child match the index cards to the items pasted in the bedroom.

9. Place the cards in an envelope and place the envelope in the child's notebook for later use.

    Exit Criteria:
        The child can match all the cards to the bedroom items in the house.

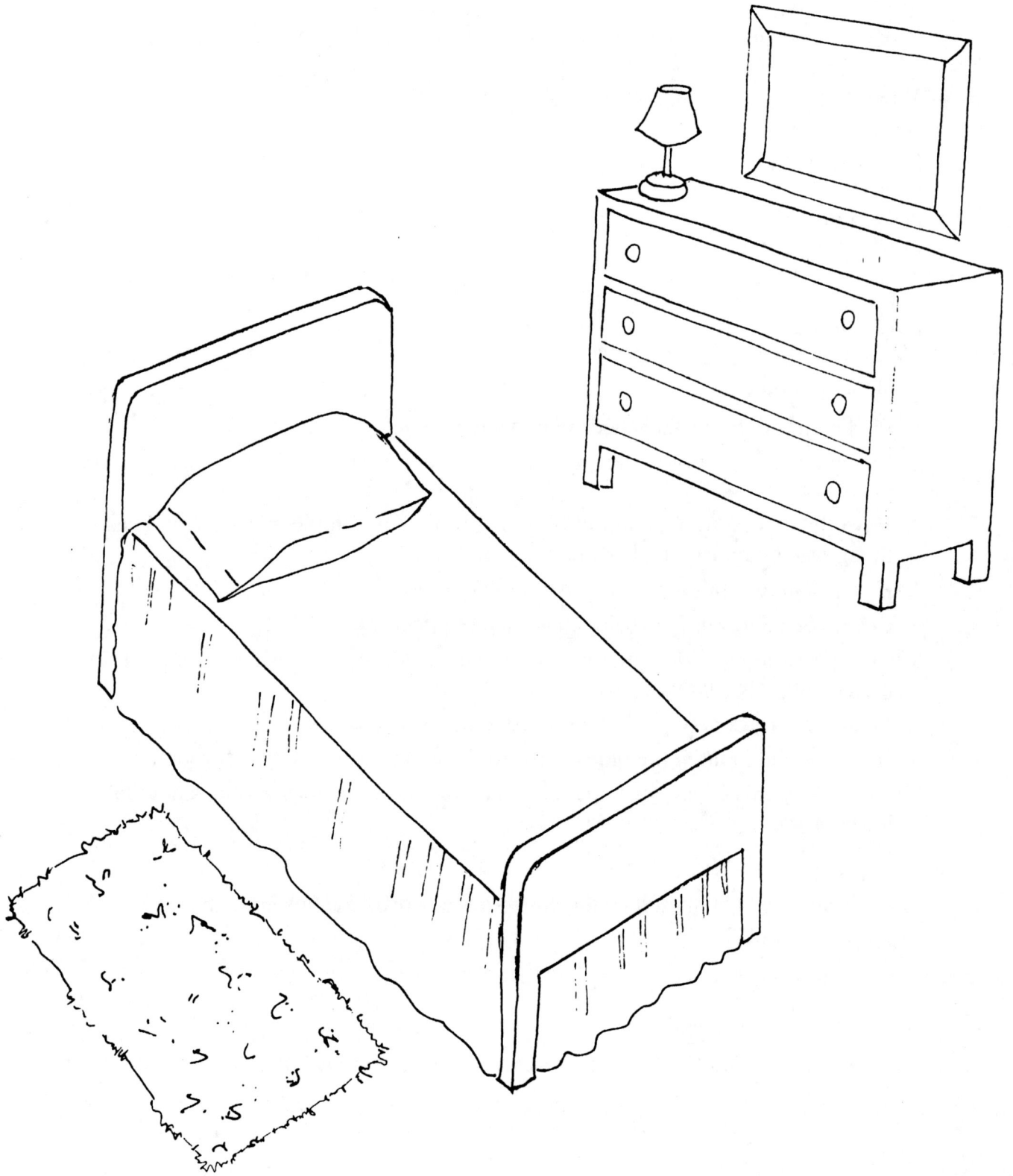

Lesson R-65

Goal: To Recognize Rooms of a House: BATHROOM

Materials:

Magazines
Lesson Illustration
Scissors
Paste/glue
Construction paper
Fabric
Index cards
Envelope

Implementation:

1. Find a picture of a bathroom in a magazine.
2. Cut out one item in the magazine bathroom and paste it into the house you've made.
3. Have the child find and cut out other bathroom items in the magazine and paste them into the house's bathroom.
4. If you wish, use fabric to make bathroom curtains.
5. Cover the bathroom floor with construction paper if desired.
6. Cut apart the individual pictures in the Lesson Illustration. Mount the pictures individually onto index cards. Label each one.
7. Match the index cards to items pasted in the bathroom.
8. Have the child match the index cards to the items pasted in the bathroom.
9. Place the cards in an envelope and place the envelope in the child's notebook for later use.

Exit Criteria:
    The child can match all the cards to the bathroom items in the house.

Lesson R-66

Goal: To Recognize Rooms of a House

Materials:

Index cards for rooms of a house from Lessons R-60 through R-65
House you've made
Magazine pictures of rooms from Lesson R-59

Implementation:

1. Have the child match all the index cards to objects in the house.
2. Lay all the cards face down. One at a time, have the child turn over the cards and find the matching furniture in the house.
3. Next, lay out the pictures of rooms from magazines from Lesson R-59 and have the child place the furniture index cards onto the appropriate magazine pictures.

   Exit Criteria:
   The child can place each item on the proper magazine room picture.

Lesson R-67

Goal: To Recognize Household Items

Materials:

House you've made
Scissors
Paste/glue

Implementation:

1. Find and cut out one item that belongs in the house from a magazine (for example, a picture for the wall). Paste the item in the house you've made.

2. Have the child find and cut out other household items. Have the child decorate the house. He may decorate the outside of the house as well.

   Exit Criteria:
       Child finds and pastes three or four items in the house.

Lesson R-68

Goal: To recognize fruits: APPLE, BANANA

Materials:

Lesson Illustration
Magazine
Color crayons
Fruit
Knife
Loose leaf paper
Paste

Implementation:

1. Cut apart the Lesson Illustration and mount each picture on an index card. One at a time, show the child the subject fruit. Tell him its name.
2. Show the child the Lesson Illustration cards and have him pick out the appropriate illustration.
3. Let the child color the picture of the fruit the appropriate color. Label the picture.
4. Have the child cut the fruit open and find the seeds, if any. Let him eat the fruit if he likes.
5. Let the child find pictures of his fruit and cut them out. Paste the pictures onto a sheet of loose leaf paper and label them.
6. Store the paper in the child's notebook.

   Exit Criteria:
   Child can find pictures of the fruits in a magazine.

APPLE

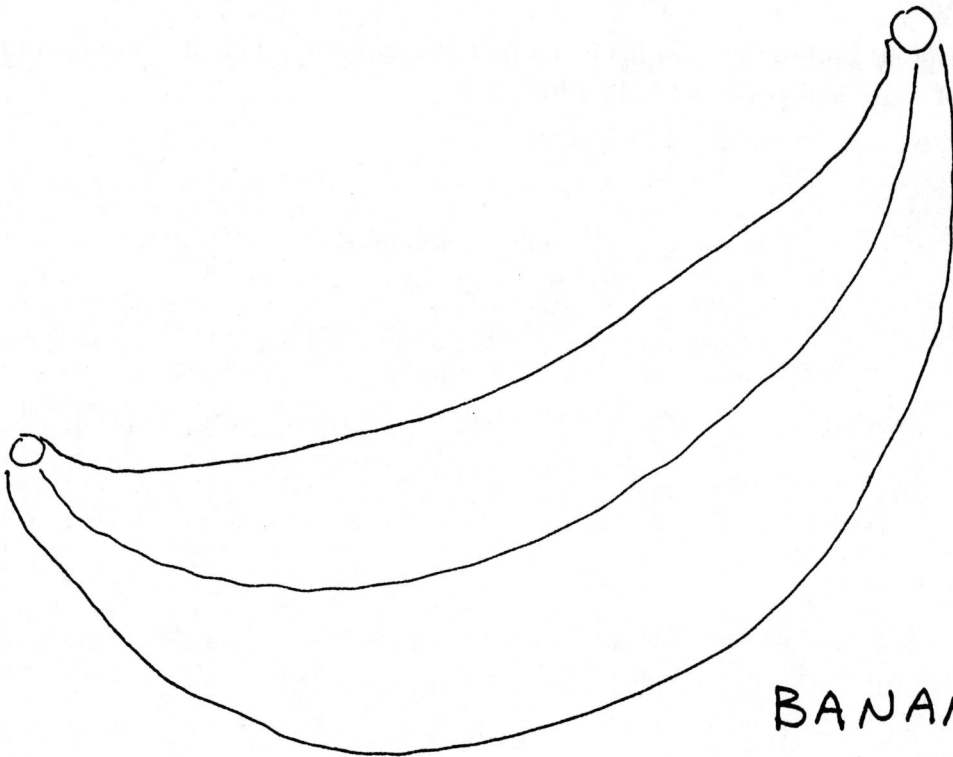

BANANA

Lesson R-69

Goal: To Recognize Fruits: CHERRY, GREEN GRAPES

Materials:

Lesson Illustration
Magazine
Color crayons
Fruit
Knife
Loose leaf paper
Paste

Implementation:

1. Cut apart the Lesson Illustration and mount each picture on an index card. One at a time, show the child the subject fruit. Tell him its name.

2. Show the child the Lesson Illustration cards and have him pick out the appropriate illustration.

3. Let the child color the picture of the fruit the appropriate color. Label the picture.

4. Have the child cut the fruit open and find the seeds, if any. Let him eat the fruit if he likes.

5. Let the child find pictures of his fruit and cut them out. Paste the pictures onto a sheet of loose leaf paper and label them.

6. Store the paper in the child's notebook.

Exit Criteria:
    Child can find pictures of the fruits in a magazine.

CHERRIES

GREEN
GRAPES

Lesson R-70

Goal: To Recognize Fruits: RED GRAPES, GRAPEFRUIT

Materials:

Lesson Illustration
Magazine
Color crayons
Fruit
Knife
Loose leaf paper
Paste

Implementation:

1. Cut apart the Lesson Illustration and mount each picture on an index card. One at a time, show the child the subject fruit. Tell him its name.

2. Show the child the Lesson Illustration cards and have him pick out the appropriate illustration.

3. Let the child color the picture of the fruit the appropriate color. Label the picture.

4. Have the child cut the fruit open and find the seeds, if any. Let him eat the fruit if he likes.

5. Let the child find pictures of his fruit and cut them out. Paste the pictures onto a sheet of loose leaf paper and label them.

6. Store the paper in the child's notebook.

Exit Criteria:
Child can find pictures of the fruits in a magazine.

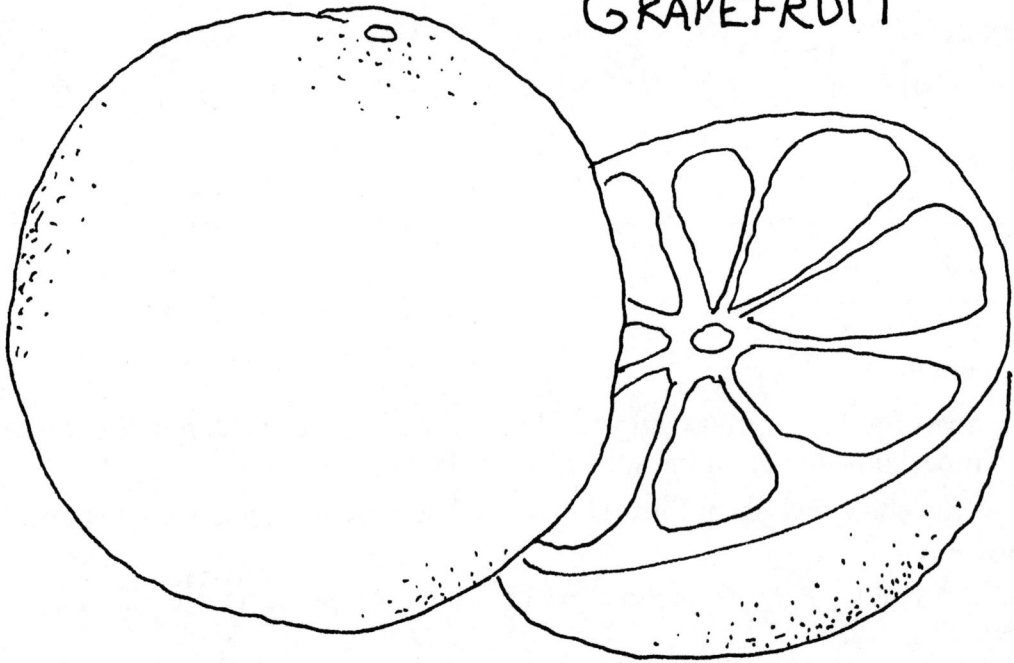

GRAPEFRUIT

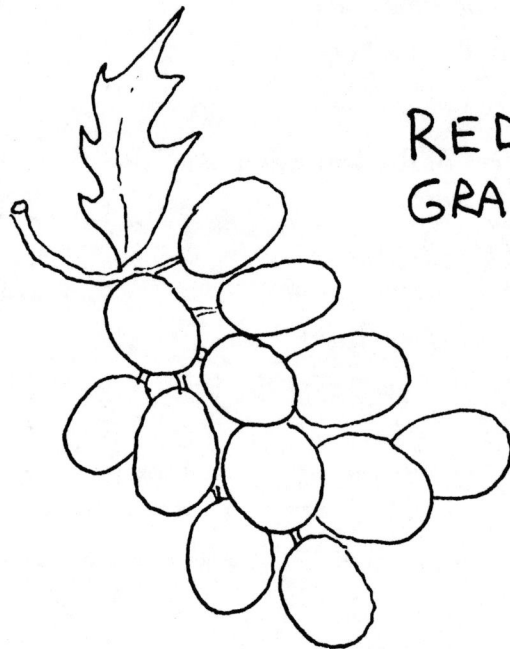

RED
GRAPES

158

Lesson R-71

Goal: To Recognize Fruits: LEMON, ORANGE

Materials:

Lesson Illustration
Magazine
Color crayons
Fruit
Knife
Loose leaf paper
Paste

Implementation:

1. Cut apart the Lesson Illustration and mount each picture on an index card. One at a time, show the child the subject fruit. Tell him its name.

2. Show the child the Lesson Illustration cards and have him pick out the appropriate illustration.

3. Let the child color the picture of the fruit the appropriate color. Label the picture.

4. Have the child cut the fruit open and find the seeds, if any. Let him eat the fruit if he likes.

5. Let the child find pictures of his fruit and cut them out. Paste the pictures onto a sheet of loose leaf paper and label them.

6. Store the paper in the child's notebook.

Exit Criteria:
Child can find pictures of the fruits in a magazine.

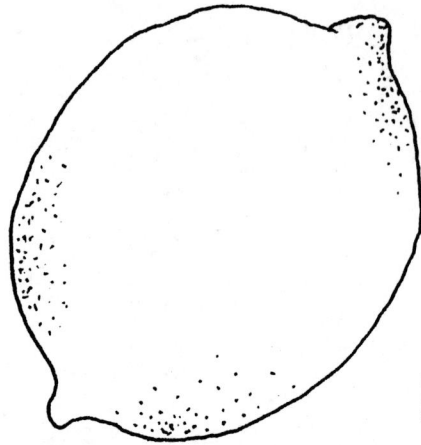

LEMON

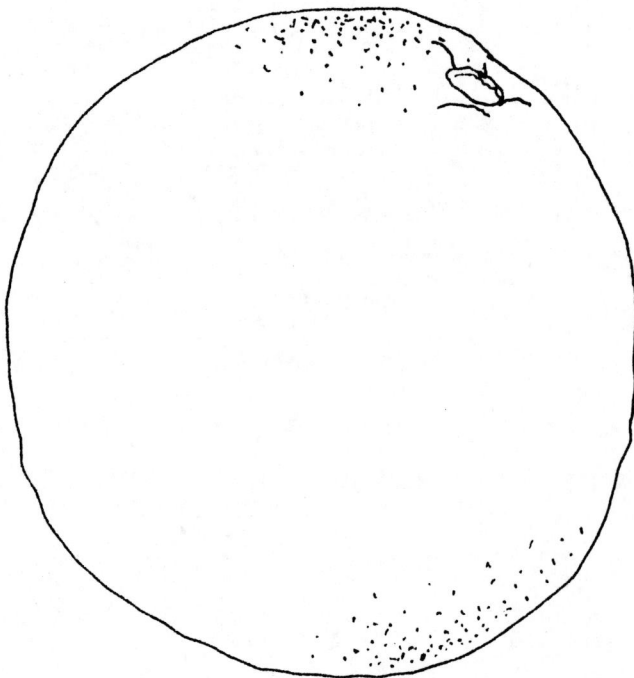

ORANGE

Lesson R-72

Goal: To Recognize Fruits: PEACH, PEAR

Materials:

Lesson Illustration
Magazine
Color crayons
Fruit
Knife
Loose leaf paper
Paste

Implementation:

1. Cut apart the Lesson Illustration and mount each picture on an index card. One at a time, show the child the subject fruit. Tell him its name.
2. Show the child the Lesson Illustration cards and have him pick out the appropriate illustration.
3. Let the child color the picture of the fruit the appropriate color. Label the picture.
4. Have the child cut the fruit open and find the seeds, if any. Let him eat the fruit if he likes.
5. Let the child find pictures of his fruit and cut them out. Paste the pictures onto a sheet of loose leaf paper and label them.
6. Store the paper in the child's notebook.

Exit Criteria:
   Child can find pictures of the fruits in a magazine.

PEACH

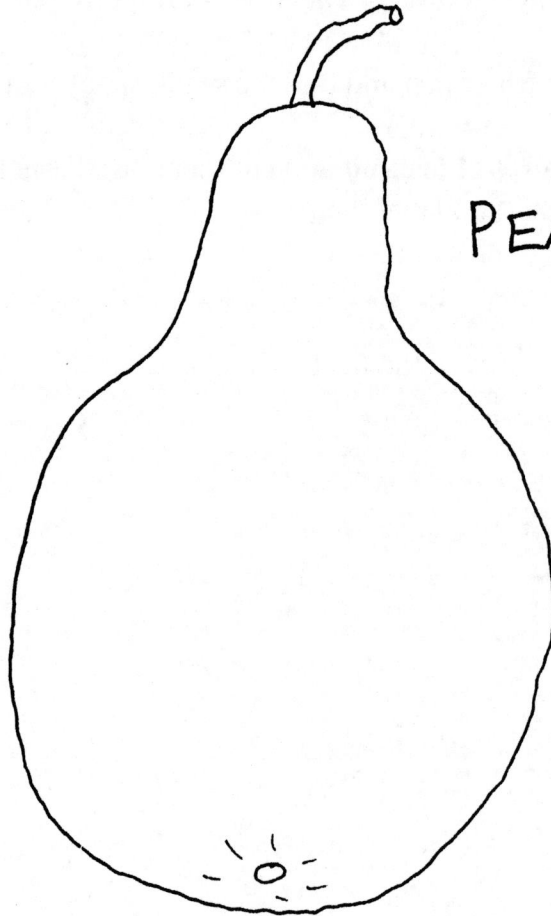

PEAR

Lesson R-73

Goal: To Recognize Fruits: PINEAPPLE, PLUM

Materials:

Lesson Illustration
Magazine
Color crayons
Fruit
Knife
Loose leaf paper
Paste

Implementation:

1. Cut apart the Lesson Illustration and mount each picture on an index card. One at a time, show the child the subject fruit. Tell him its name.

2. Show the child the Lesson Illustration cards and have him pick out the appropriate illustration.

3. Let the child color the picture of the fruit the appropriate color. Label the picture.

4. Have the child cut the fruit open and find the seeds, if any. Let him eat the fruit if he likes.

5. Let the child find pictures of his fruit and cut them out. Paste the pictures onto a sheet of loose leaf paper and label them.

6. Store the paper in the child's notebook.

Exit Criteria:
    Child can find pictures of the fruits in a magazine.

PINEAPPLE

PLUM

Lesson R-74

Goal: To Recognize Fruits: STRAWBERRY, BLUEBERRY

Materials:

Lesson Illustration
Magazine
Color crayons
Fruit
Knife
Loose leaf paper
Paste

Implementation:

1. Cut apart the Lesson Illustration and mount each picture on an index card. One at a time, show the child the subject fruit. Tell him its name.

2. Show the child the Lesson Illustration cards and have him pick out the appropriate illustration.

3. Let the child color the picture of the fruit the appropriate color. Label the picture.

4. Have the child cut the fruit open and find the seeds, if any. Let him eat the fruit if he likes.

5. Let the child find pictures of his fruit and cut them out. Paste the pictures onto a sheet of loose leaf paper and label them.

6. Store the paper in the child's notebook.

   Exit Criteria:
       Child can find pictures of the fruits in a magazine.

STRAWBERRY

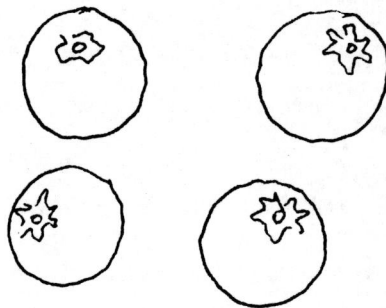

BLUEBERRY

Lesson R-75

Goal: To Recognize Fruits: TANGERINE, LIME

Materials:

Lesson Illustration
Magazine
Color crayons
Fruit
Knife
Loose leaf paper
Paste

Implementation:

1. Cut apart the Lesson Illustration and mount each picture on an index card. One at a time, show the child the subject fruit. Tell him its name.

2. Show the child the Lesson Illustration cards and have him pick out the appropriate illustration.

3. Let the child color the picture of the fruit the appropriate color. Label the picture.

4. Have the child cut the fruit open and find the seeds, if any. Let him eat the fruit if he likes.

5. Let the child find pictures of his fruit and cut them out. Paste the pictures onto a sheet of loose leaf paper and label them.

6. Store the paper in the child's notebook.

Exit Criteria:
    Child can find pictures of the fruits in a magazine.

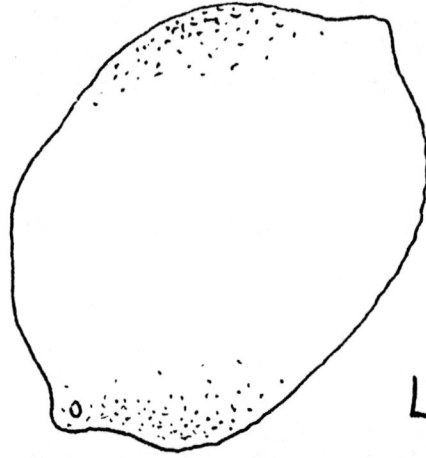

LIME

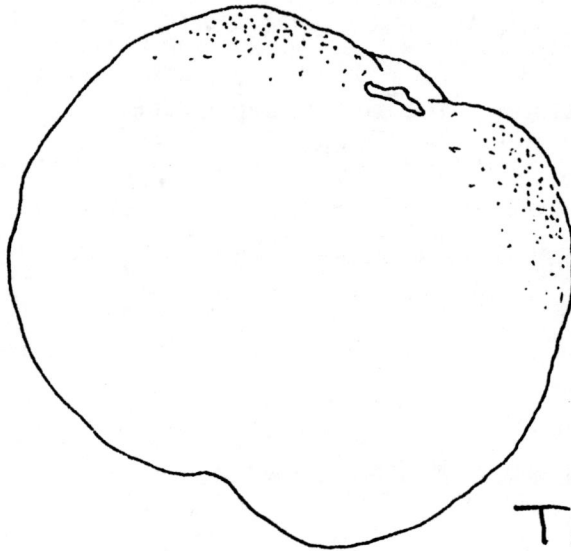

TANGERINE

Lesson R-76

Goal: To Recognize All Sixteen Fruits

Materials:

Lesson Illustrations R-68—R-75
Lesson Illustration cards from Lessons R-68—R-75
Paste/glue
Scissors
Sixteen index cards
Notebook

Implementation:

1. Have the child help you cut apart the pictures in the Lesson Illustrations and mount them onto the index cards.
2. Take the sixteen fruit pictures the child has colored and mounted in the previous lessons. Take one picture at a time and have the child find in his notebook the matching fruit picture that he cut out of the magazine.
3. Name each fruit as the child matches his picture to the magazine picture.
4. After he has matched all the cards to the pictures, lay the two sets of index cards face down and play "Concentration."

   Exit Criteria:
   Child matches all the cards to the pictures in notebook.

Lesson R-77

Goal: To Recognize Vegetables: GREEN BEANS, TOMATO

Materials:

Lesson Illustration
Magazine
Color crayons
Paper
Vegetable
Knife
Loose leaf paper
Paste/glue

Implementation:

1. Cut apart the Lesson Illustration and mount each picture on an index card.
2. Show the child the vegetable and tell him its name.
3. Show the child the Lesson Illustration cards and have him pick out the appropriate illustration.
4. Let the child color the picture of the vegetable the appropriate color. Label the picture.
5. Have the child cut the vegetable open and examine it. Let him eat the vegetable if he likes.
6. Let the child find pictures of the vegetable and cut them out. Paste the pictures onto a sheet of looseleaf paper and label them.

Exit Criteria:
   Child can find pictures of the vegetable in the magazine.

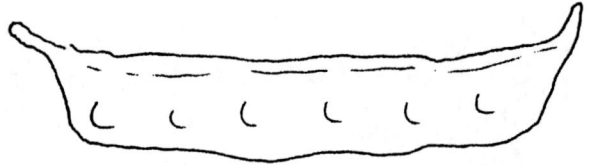

GREEN BEANS

TOMATO

Lesson R-78

Goal: To Recognize Vegetables: CARROTS, CELERY

Materials:

Lesson Illustration
Magazine
Color crayons
Paper
Vegetable
Knife
Loose leaf paper
Paste/glue

Implementation:

1. Cut apart the Lesson Illustration and mount each picture on an index card.
2. Show the child the vegetable and tell him its name.
3. Show the child the Lesson Illustration cards and have him pick out the appropriate illustration.
4. Let the child color the picture of the vegetable the appropriate color. Label the picture.
5. Have the child cut the vegetable open and examine it. Let him eat the vegetable if he likes.
6. Let the child find pictures of the vegetable and cut them out. Paste the pictures onto a sheet of looseleaf paper and label them.

Exit Criteria:
   Child can find pictures of the vegetable in the magazine.

CARROTS

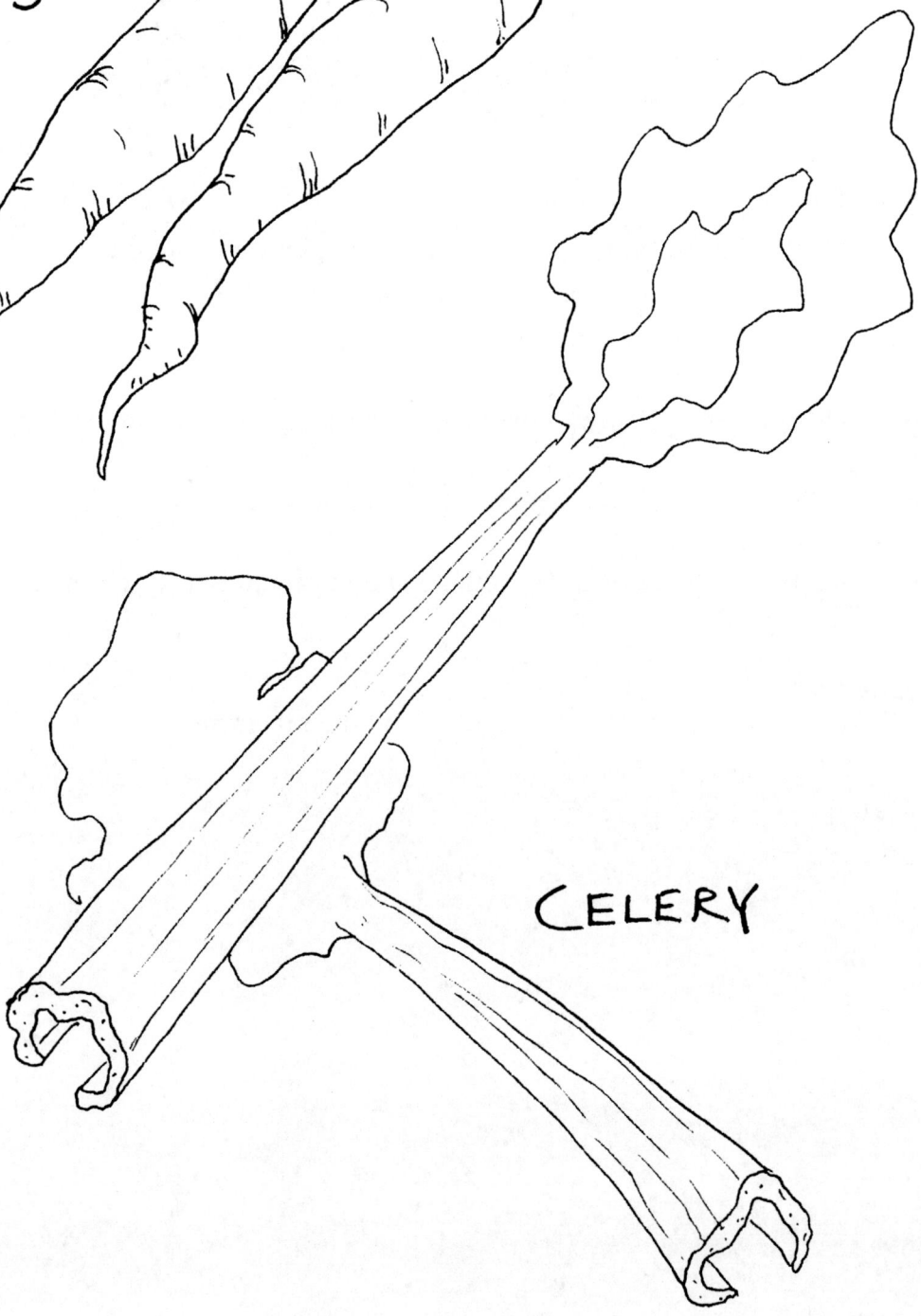

CELERY

Lesson R-79

Goal: To Recognize Vegetables: CUCUMBER, LETTUCE

Materials:

Lesson Illustration
Magazine
Color crayons
Paper
Vegetable
Knife
Loose leaf paper
Paste/glue

Implementation:

1. Cut apart the Lesson Illustration and mount each picture on an index card.

2. Show the child the vegetable and tell him its name.

3. Show the child the Lesson Illustration cards and have him pick out the appropriate illustration.

4. Let the child color the picture of the vegetable the appropriate color. Label the picture.

5. Have the child cut the vegetable open and examine it. Let him eat the vegetable if he likes.

6. Let the child find pictures of the vegetable and cut them out. Paste the pictures onto a sheet of looseleaf paper and label them.

   Exit Criteria:
   Child can find pictures of the vegetable in the magazine.

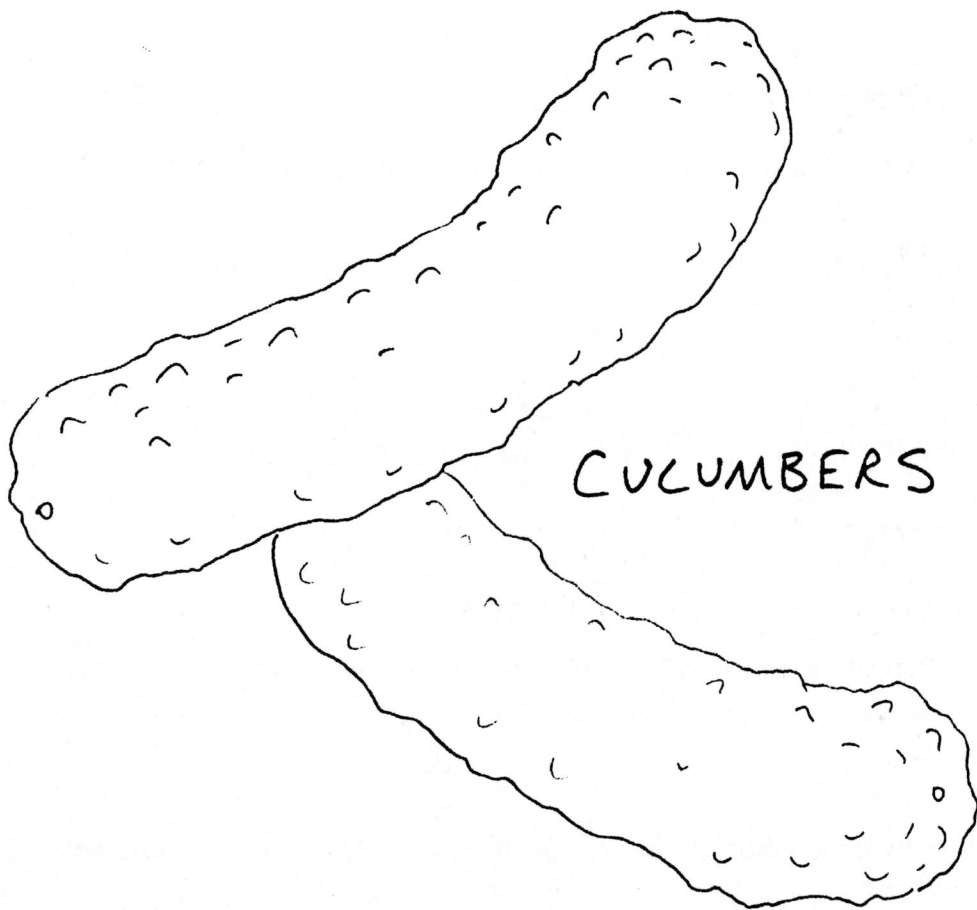

CUCUMBERS

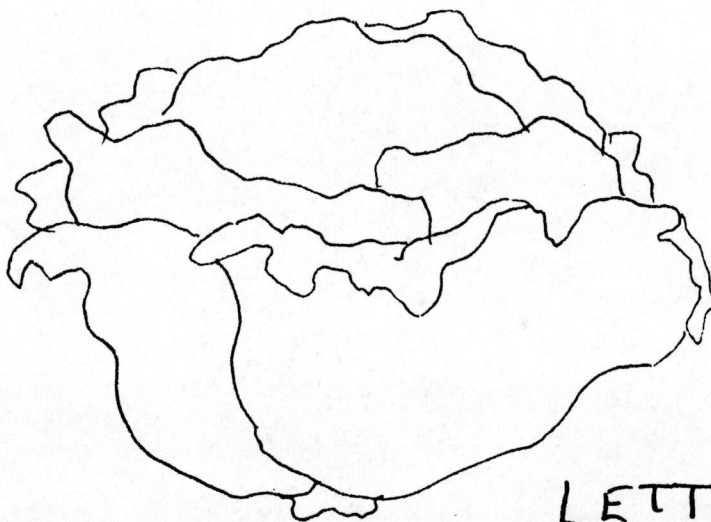

LETTUCE

Lesson R-80

Goal: To Recognize Vegetables: ONIONS, GREEN PEPPERS

Materials:

Lesson Illustration
Magazine
Color crayons
Paper
Vegetable
Knife
Loose leaf paper
Paste/glue

Implementation:

1. Cut apart the Lesson Illustration and mount each picture on an index card.

2. Show the child the vegetable and tell him its name.

3. Show the child the Lesson Illustration cards and have him pick out the appropriate illustration.

4. Let the child color the picture of the vegetable the appropriate color. Label the picture.

5. Have the child cut the vegetable open and examine it. Let him eat the vegetable if he likes.

6. Let the child find pictures of the vegetable and cut them out. Paste the pictures onto a sheet of looseleaf paper and label them.

Exit Criteria:
    Child can find pictures of the vegetable in the magazine.

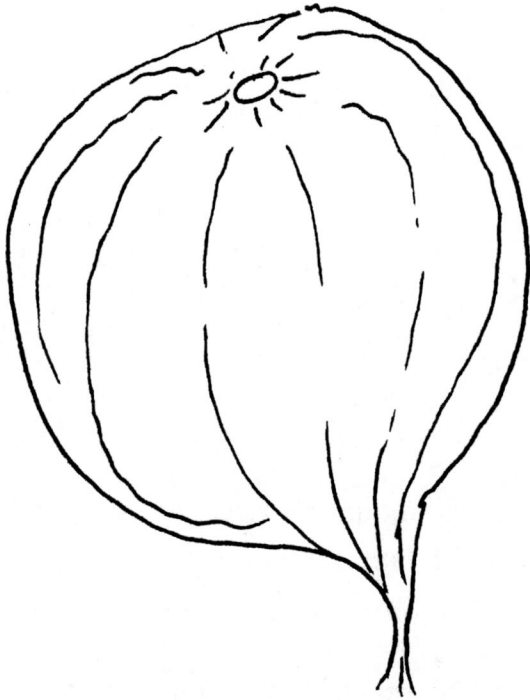

ONION

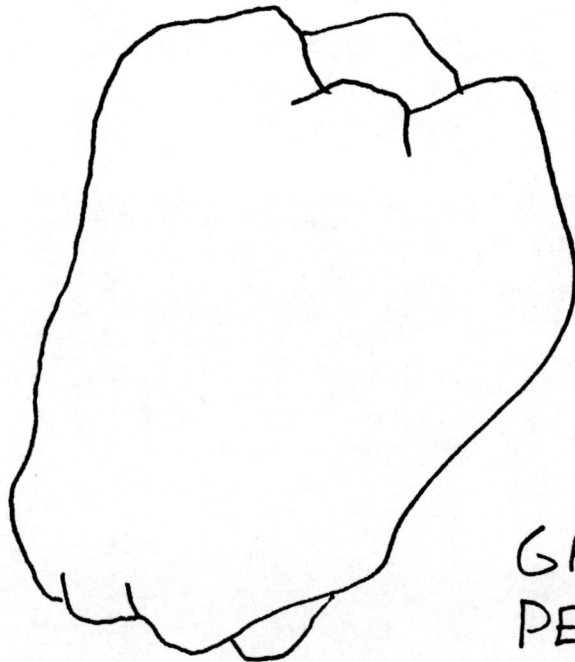

GREEN
PEPPER

Lesson R-81

Goal: To Recognize Vegetables: PARSLEY, RADISH

Materials:

Lesson Illustration
Magazine
Color crayons
Paper
Vegetable
Knife
Loose leaf paper
Paste/glue

Implementation:

1. Cut apart the Lesson Illustration and mount each picture on an index card.
2. Show the child the vegetable and tell him its name.
3. Show the child the Lesson Illustration cards and have him pick out the appropriate illustration.
4. Let the child color the picture of the vegetable the appropriate color. Label the picture.
5. Have the child cut the vegetable open and examine it. Let him eat the vegetable if he likes.
6. Let the child find pictures of the vegetable and cut them out. Paste the pictures onto a sheet of looseleaf paper and label them.

Exit Criteria:
    Child can find pictures of the vegetable in the magazine.

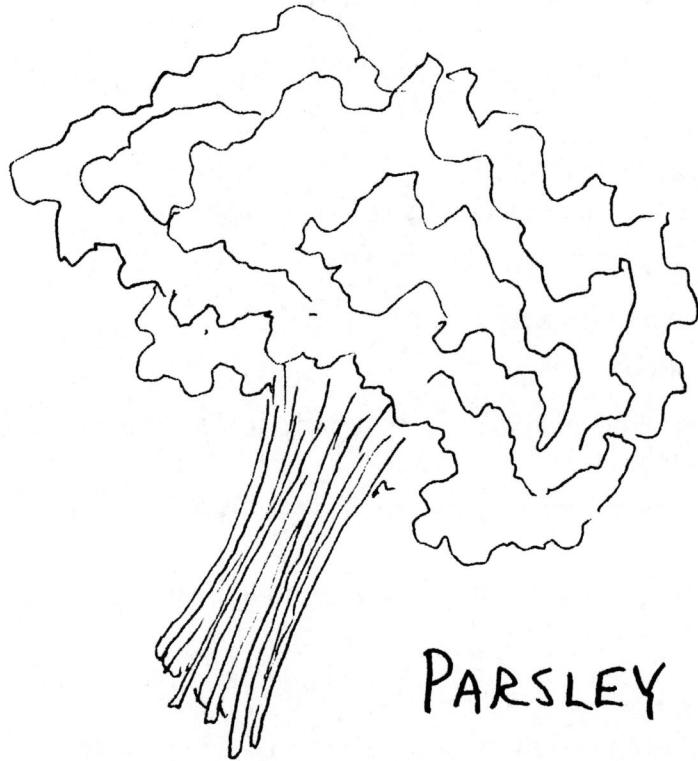

PARSLEY

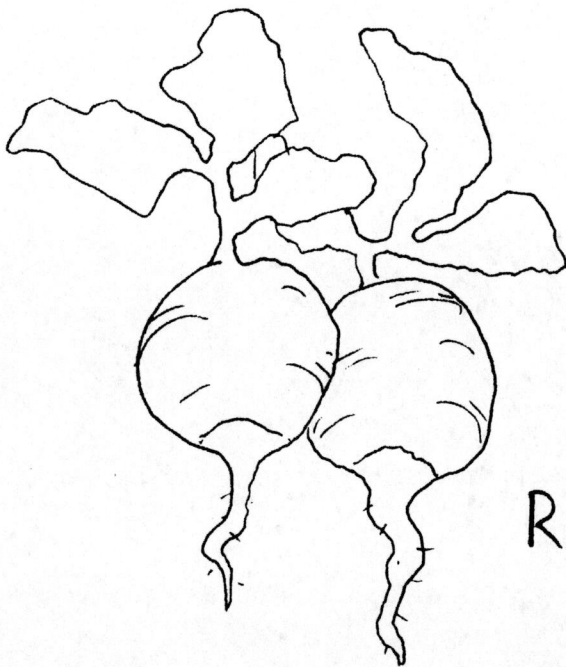

RADISH

Lesson R-82

Goal: To Recognize Vegetables: SALAD

Materials:

Bean sprouts (if available)
Other vegetables as desired
Vegetable index cards from Lessons R-77—R-81
Bowl
Forks
Salad dressing, if desired

Implementation:

1. Have the child match each vegetable to its index card. Name each vegetable as he matches it.

2. Tell the child, "We are going to make a *salad*." Help the child chop or cut up the vegetables.

3. Put the vegetables into the bowl and make a salad. Enjoy the salad with the child.

Exit Criteria:
    Child can match five vegetables to their pictures.

Lesson R-83

Goal: To Recognize Spring Activities

Materials:

Color crayons
Magazines
Scissors
Loose leaf paper
Paste/glue

Implementation:

1. Label a piece of paper, "SPRING." Look through the magazines and find pictures of spring activities.

2. Cut them out and paste them onto the SPRING sheet.

3. Have the child find pictures of spring clothing, animals, flowers, etc., in the magazines.

4. Cut out all the pictures the child finds and paste them onto the SPRING sheet.

5. Put the SPRING sheet in the child's notebook.

Exit Criteria:
    Child can find two pictures from each category listed above.

Lesson R-84

Goal: To Recognize Summer Activities

Materials:
Color crayons
Magazines
Scissors
Loose leaf paper
Paste/glue

Implementation:

1. Label a piece of paper, "SUMMER." Look through the magazines and find pictures of summer activities.
2. Cut them out and paste them onto the SUMMER sheet.
3. Have the child find pictures of summer clothing, animals, flowers, etc., in the magazines.
4. Cut out all the pictures the child finds and paste them onto the SUMMER sheet.
5. Put the SUMMER sheet in the child's notebook.

Exit Criteria:
Child can find two pictures from each category listed above.

Lesson R-85

Goal: To Recognize Fall Activities

Materials:

Color crayons
Magazines
Scissors
Loose leaf paper
Paste/glue

Implementation:

1. Label a piece of paper "FALL." Look through the magazines and find pictures of fall activities.
2. Cut them out and paste them onto the FALL sheet.
3. Have the child find pictures of fall clothing, animals, plants, etc., in the magazines.
4. Cut out all the pictures the child finds and paste them on the FALL sheet.
5. Put the FALL sheet in the child's notebook.

   Exit Criteria:
   Child can find two pictures from each category listed above.

Lesson R-86

Goal: To Recognize Winter Activities

Materials:

Color crayons
Magazines
Scissors
Loose leaf paper
Paste/glue

Implementation:

1. Label a piece of paper, "WINTER." Look through the magazines and find pictures of winter activities.

2. Cut them out and paste them onto the WINTER sheet.

3. Have the child find pictures of winter clothing, animals, plants, etc., in the magazines.

4. Cut out all the pictures the child finds and paste them on the WINTER sheet.

5. Put the WINTER sheet in the child's notebook.

Exit Criteria:
   Child can find two pictures from each category listed above.

Lesson R-87

Goal: To Discuss Birthdays*

Materials:

Lesson Illustration
Color crayons
Paste
Scissors

Implementation:

1. Sing "Happy Birthday" to the child.
2. Have the child tell you how old he is.
3. Show the child the Lesson Illustration and have him count the candles that he needs to show how old he is.
4. Have the child color the cake and cut out the appropriate number candles.
5. Paste the candles on the cake.
6. Talk about birthdays and if possible, continue the celebration with a real cake or cupcake and the appropriate number of candles. Have the child count the real candles to make sure there are the right number.

   Exit Criteria:
   The child must be able to tell you how old he is, and to designate and cut out the appropriate number of candles.

*For use on the child's birthday.

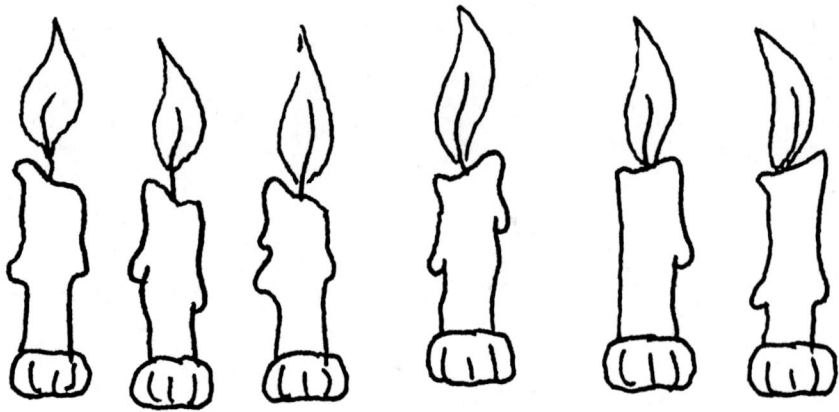

Lesson R-88

Goal: To Discuss Halloween

Materials:

Color crayons
Lesson Illustration
Scissors
String

Implementation:

1. Talk to the child about Halloween. Discuss the date of Halloween and find it on the calendar. Have the child tell you what he will do on Halloween.

2. Look at the Lesson Illustrations and have the child describe what is on them.

3. Have the child follow the directions of the Lesson Illustration with the three pumpkins.

4. If time permits, have the child color the masks and cut them out.

Exit Criteria:

The child is able to find Halloween on the calendar. He must be able to tell you what he did on the Lesson Illustrations.

Make two happy
Jack-o-lantern faces and
one sad Jack-o-lantern face

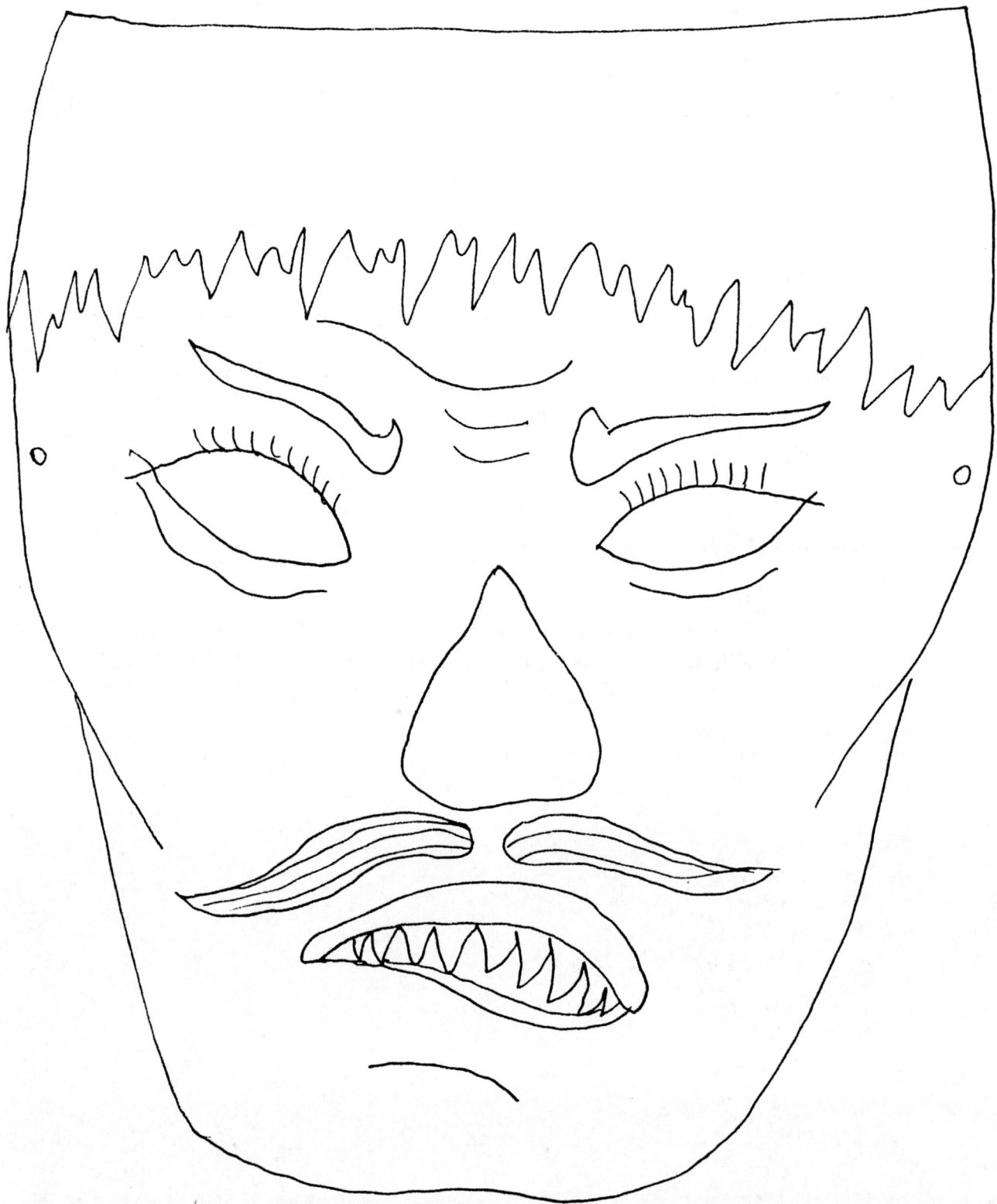

Lesson R-89

Goal: To Discuss Halloween

Materials:

Color crayons
Paper
Candy
Bag

Implementation:

1. Have the child draw a picture of what he will look like on Halloween dressed up in his costume.

2. Ask him to tell you what he will do. Elicit the response, "Trick or treat."

3. Review the proper way to trick or treat:

   The child knocks on the door or rings the doorbell.
   When someone opens the door, he says, "Trick or treat."
   When the child is given candy, he says, "Thank you."

4. Have the child practice trick-or-treating with you.

   Exit Criteria:
   The child is able to say "Trick or treat" and "Thank you" appropriately.
   He must be able to tell you what type of costume he will wear.

Lesson R-90

Goal: To Discuss Thanksgiving

Materials:

A book about Thanksgiving

Implementation:

1. Read the book to the child OR tell the child the story of Thanksgiving:

   The Pilgrims came across the ocean and settled in a new land, America.
   The Pilgrims made friends with the Indians.
   The Pilgrims planted food and the Indians helped them.
   The food grew and the Pilgrims were happy.
   The Indians and the Pilgrims had a big dinner.
   They all said "Thank you" to God.

   Exit Criteria:
      The child is able to tell you the sequence of at least three events listed above.

Lesson R-91

Goal: To Discuss Thanksgiving

Materials:

Lesson Illustration
Color crayons
Notebook

Implementation:

1. Have the child color the picture of the turkey.

2. Ask the child to tell you what he will do over the Thanksgiving break.

3. Review the names of the members of the child's family and have the child tell you who will be having Thanksgiving dinner with him.

4. Put the picture of the turkey in the child's notebook.

Exit Criteria:
   The child is able to identify the turkey. He must be able to name the members of his family.

Lesson R-92

Goal: To Discuss Christmas

Materials:

Lesson Illustration
Color crayons
Notebook
Paste/glue
Scissors

Implementation:

1. Ask the child to tell you about the pictures in the Lesson Illustration.
2. Have him name what the pictures represent. Make sure he can identify the Christmas tree, the ornaments and Santa Claus.
3. Have the child color the ornaments and tree. After he has finished, have him name the colors of the ornaments and count them.
4. Cut out the pieces to be used to make Santa. Let the child color the pieces appropriately.
5. Have the child watch while you follow the directions to make the Santa. Discuss each step with the child as you do it.
6. Have the child repeat back to you the steps you took to make the Santa.

Exit Criteria:
   The child is able to name the colors used to color the ornaments. He is able to count the ornaments. He is able to sequence the actions needed to make the Santa.

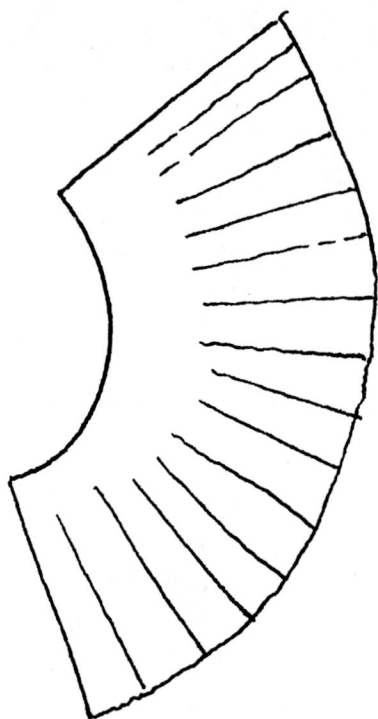

Color on both sides.
Cut out Santa and beard.
Fringe beard on lines and
  paste on face at dotted lir

Cut slits on both ends an
  interlock to form cylinder
Paste large blob of cotto
  on end of cap and ben
  back to rest on standi
  surface.

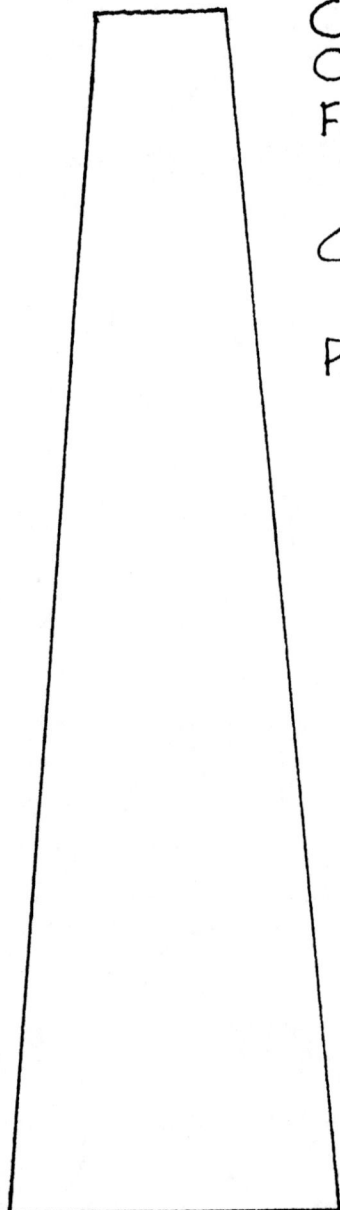

Lesson R-93

Goal: To Discuss Christmas

Materials:

Lesson Illustration
Stand up Santa from Lesson R-92

Implementation:

1. Show the child the Lesson Illustration. Ask the child what you will be making. Elicit the response, "A beard."

2. Ask the child to find the beard on the Santa you made in Lesson R-92 and have the child name the parts of Santa's face.

3. Make the beard as the child watches you.

4. Have the child tell you about Santa Claus. For instance,

He wears a red suit.
He is very jolly.
He likes good boys and girls.
He comes at Christmastime.
He rides a sleigh.
He makes toys.
He says "Ho Ho Ho!"

Exit Criteria:
    The child is able to name the parts of Santa's face in a sentence:
        Beard
        Eyes
        Nose
        Mouth
The child is able to tell you four things about Santa Claus.

Cut out on heavy lines.
Fringe beard and mustache
on light lines.
Place bows over ears.

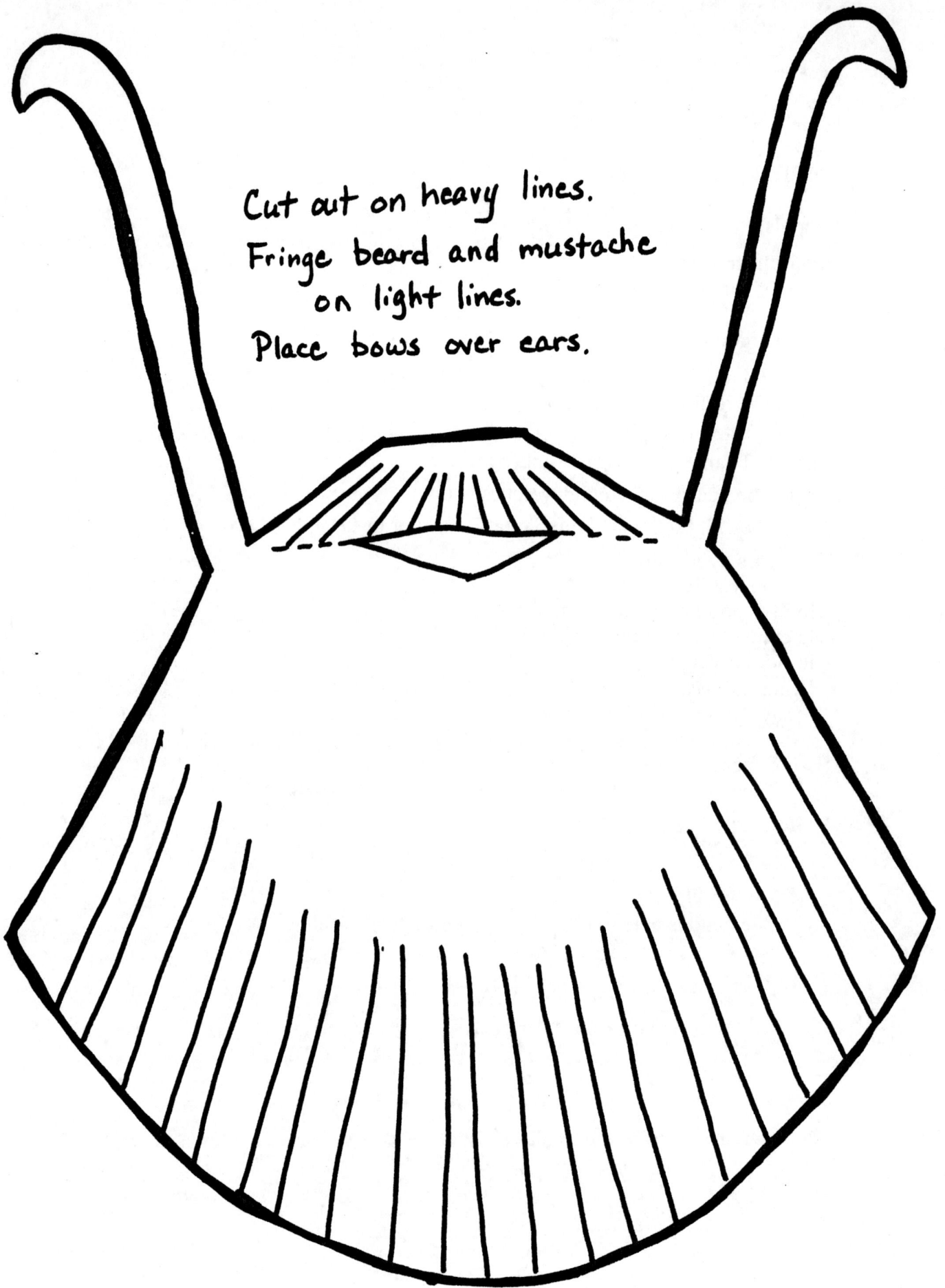

Lesson R-94

Goal: To Discuss Christmas

Materials:

Lesson Illustration
Color crayons

Implementation:

1. Bring out the Lesson Illustration showing Santa at the work bench.

2. Ask the child to tell you about the picture. Ask him such questions as:

   Who is sitting down?
   What is he doing?
   What is Santa making?
   What items are on the workbench?

3. Have the child tell you about the second Lesson Illustration. Ask him the following questions:

   How many balls are there? (3)
   How many toy animals? (5)
   How many clowns? (2)
   How many dolls? (3)
   How many toy soldiers? (1)
   What kinds of animals are there?
   How many toys are on the top shelf? (5)
   How many toys are on the middle shelf? (4)
   How many toys are on the bottom shelf? (4)
   How many toys are on the floor? (1)

   Exit Criteria:
        The child is able to answer all the questions.

Lesson R-95

Goal: To Discuss Christmas

Materials:

Two copies of Lesson Illustration

Implementation:

1. Cut apart one copy of the Lesson Illustration.
2. Have the child look at one picture at a time and name each item pictured.
3. Have the child tell you one thing about each picture. (For example, "Candy canes taste good." "The bells ring.")
4. Play Lotto with the pictures and the second copy of the Lesson Illustration.

   Exit Criteria:

   The child is able to name all items pictured and tell you one thing about each one.

Santa Claus	Bells	Caroler

Wreath	Christmas Tree	Candy Canes
		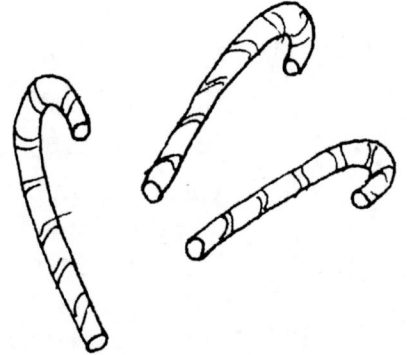

Sleigh	Present	Toys
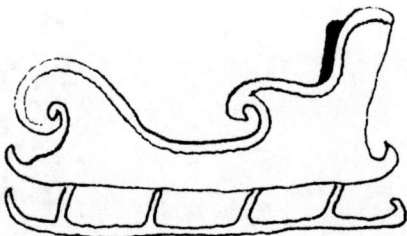		

Lesson R-96

Goal: To Discuss Valentine's Day

Materials:

Red paper squares
White paper squares (smaller than the red squares)
Scissors
Paste/glue
Color crayons

Implementation:

1. Tell the child that you are going to make a Valentine. Tell him to watch what you are doing so that he can do it too.

2. Proceed as follows. Narrate each step as you do it.
    A. "First, I will fold the red paper in half and draw half a heart on it."
    B. "Next, I will cut it out."
    C. "I will fold the white paper in half and draw the same thing on it."
    D. "Now I will cut it out."
    E. "I will open both papers. I have a big red heart and a small white heart."
    F. "I will paste the small heart on the big heart. Now, I have a Valentine."

3. Have the child make a Valentine, following the same procedure. Re-state the steps for him when necessary. If necessary, draw the design on his paper. Encourage the child to tell you what he is doing as he does it.

Exit Criteria:
    The child is able to sequence and narrate the activity.

Lesson R-97

Goal: To Discuss Easter

Materials:

Lesson Illustration
Color crayons
Scissors

Implementation:

1. Have the child color the large Easter egg.

2. Have him tell you what color he made it.

3. Have the child count the small Easter eggs.

4. Have him color as many as he can count.

5. Have the child color the Easter basket.

6. While the child is coloring the basket, cut out the eggs he colored.

7. Have the child ask you for the eggs by description. Give him each egg he describes correctly and let him paste them in the basket.

8. Put the pictures in the child's notebook.

Exit Criteria:
    The child is able to tell you what color he colored the large egg. He is able to count seven eggs. He is able to request eggs by color.

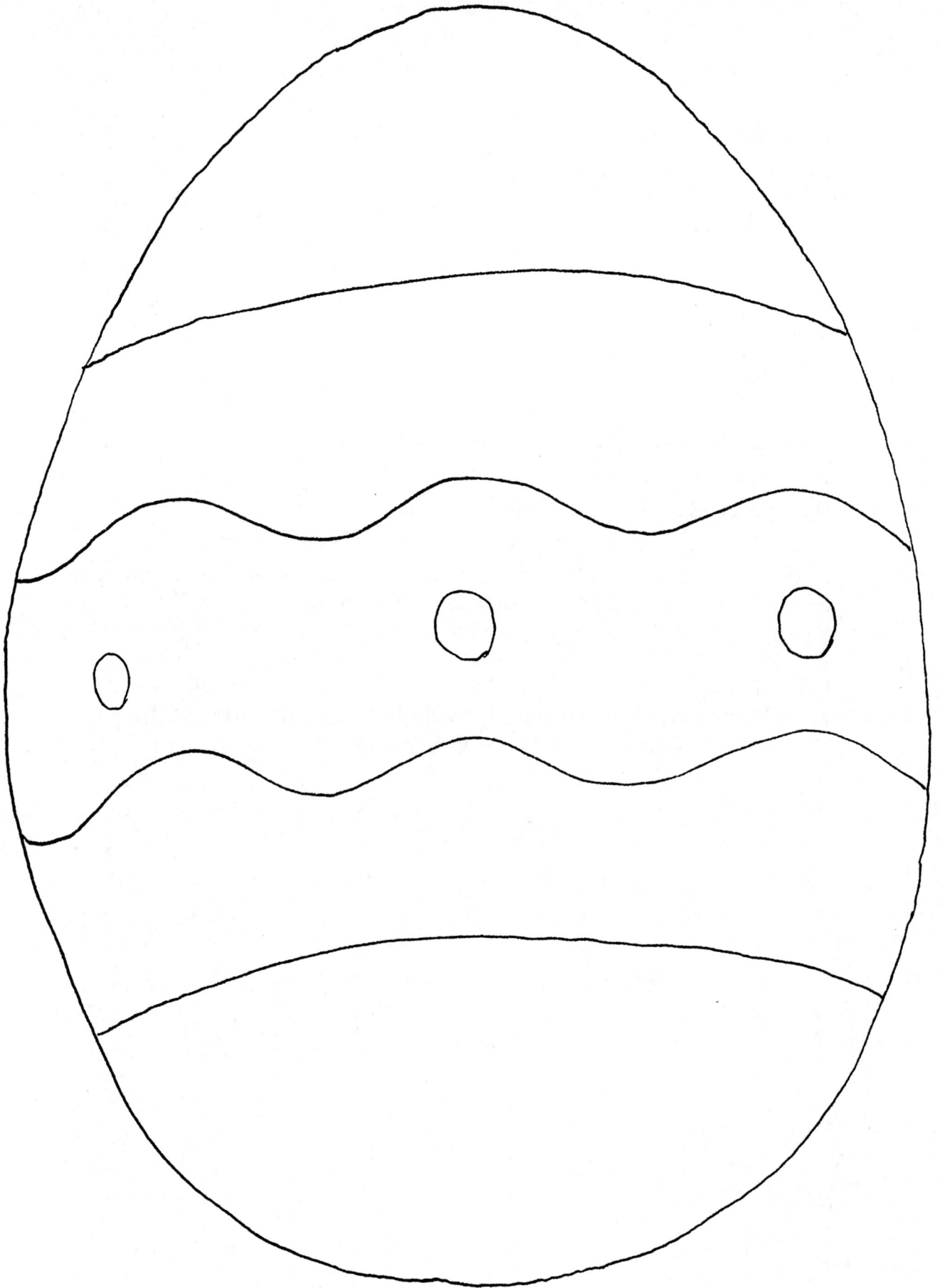

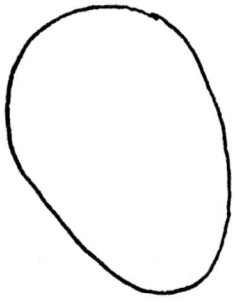

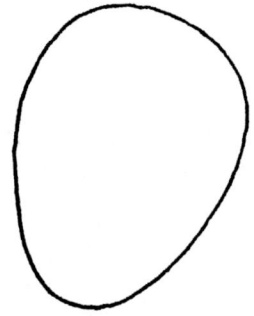

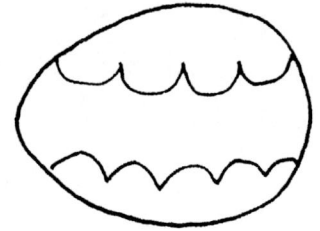

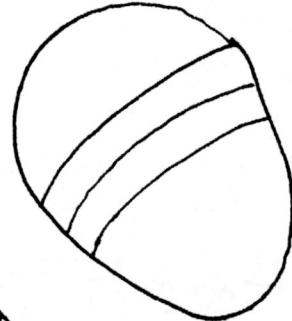

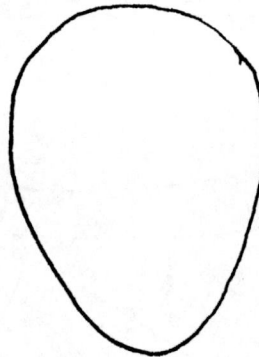
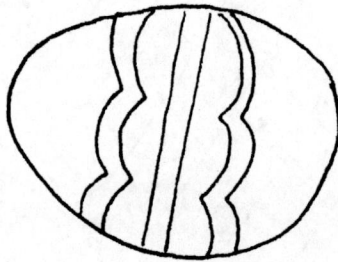
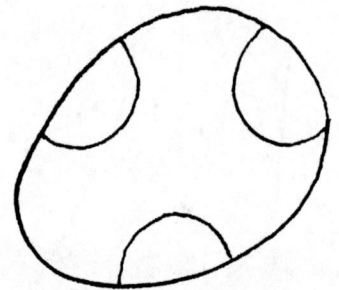

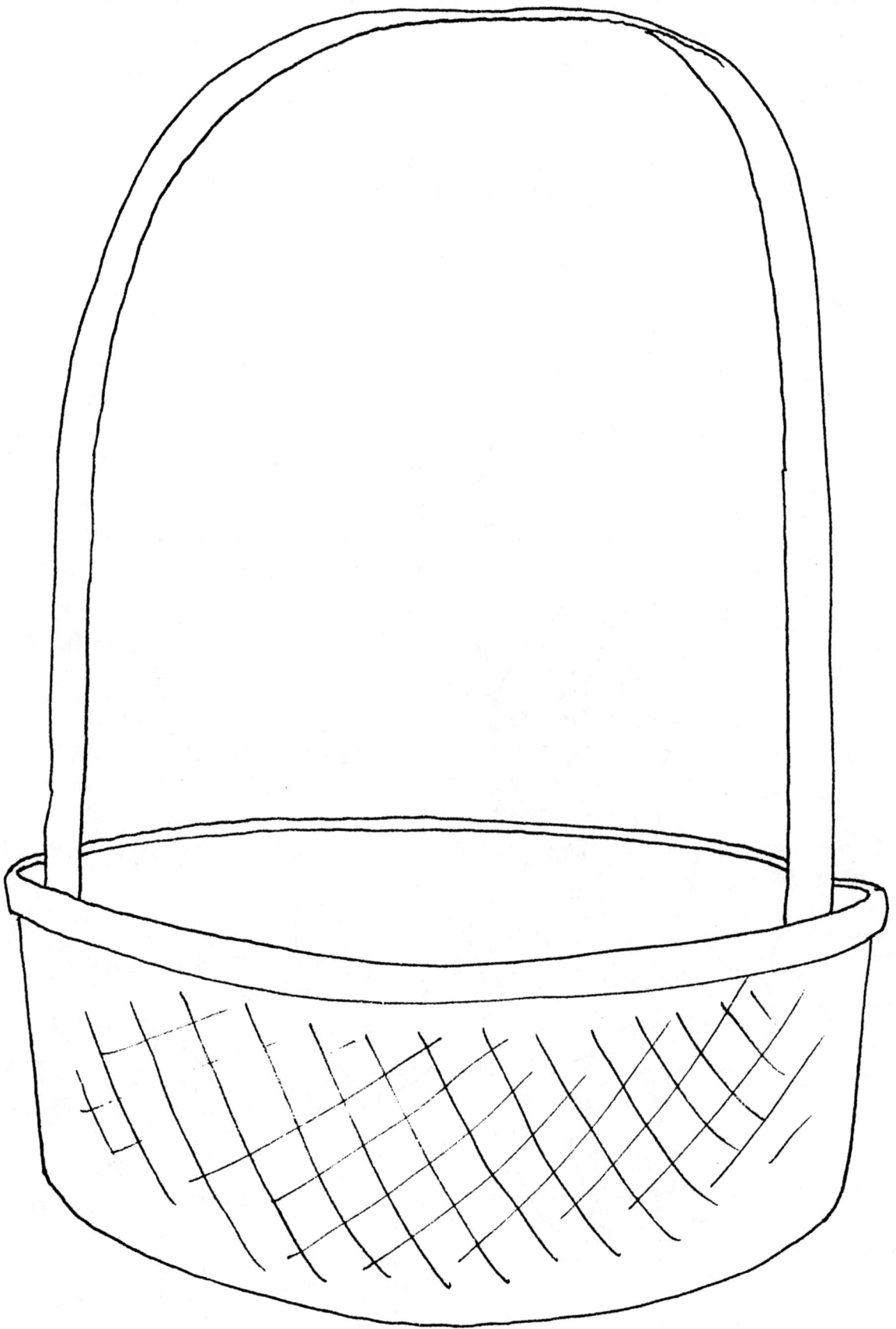

WE'LL HELP YOU TO HELP THEM.

EDUCATION

108-80 LOOKING AT CHILDREN. Richard Goldman, Ph.D. Johanne Peck, Ph.D.; Stephen Lehane, Ed.D. Combines theory and practice, exploring such issues as language development, classification, play and moral development in children. Also includes a look at sex typing, television, single-parent families, and the fathers role in parenting. **$12.95**

407-80 ALTERNATIVE APPROACHES TO EDUCATING YOUNG CHILDREN. Martha Abbott, Ph.D.; Brenda Galina, Ph.D.; Robert Granger, Ph.D., Barry Klein, Ph.D. Delves into the theoretical basis behind three major programmatic approaches to education: programs emphasizing skill development; cognitive growth; and affective development. This book encourages the reader to develop his or her own theoretical and philosophical position. Each approach is discussed according to rationale and Philosophy, Curriculum Goals, Planning of Instruction, Use of Physical Space, Instructional Materials, Evaluation Methods, and the Instructional Role of the Teacher and Child. **$6.95**

413-80 YOUNG CHILDREN'S BEHAVIOR. Johanne Peck, Ph.D. Approaches to discipline and guidance to help the readers deal more effectively with young children. Six units focus on "Examining Your Goals," "Looking At Behavior," "Young Children's Views of Right, Wrong and Rules," "Applying Behavior Modification," and "Supporting Childs Needs." **$7.95**

406-80 THE WHOLE TEACHER. Kathy R. Thornburg, Ph.D. Designed for education majors and teachers of early childhood programs, this book presents a unified approach to teacher training. Topics addressed include: personal attitues, curriculum planning and development; classroom management techniques; working with volunteers, staff and parents; and professional development. **$12.95**

418-80 ORIENTATION TO PRE-SCHOOL ASSESSMENT. T. Thomas McMurrain. Designed for the child development center staff, this handbook presents a clear description of the effective assessment of the individual child. In addition, this manual is the user's guide to HUMANICS CHILD DEVELOPMENT ASSESSMENT FORM, a developmental checklist of skills and behavior that normally emerge during the 3 to 6 year range. Includes 5 assessment tools. **$14.95**

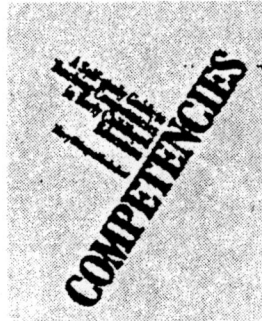

419A-80 COMPETENCIES: A SELF STUDY GUIDE FOR TEACHING COMPETENCIES IN EARLY CHILDHOOD. Mary E. Kasindorf. Divided into six competency areas and thirteen functional areas of competence as identified by the Child Development Consortium. This guide can be used to identify existing teaching skills and training needs. Designed to serve as an aid for those preparing for the C.D.A. credential. It contains checklists of teacher and child behaviors and activities that would indicate competence and can be used in assembling a C.D.A. portfolio. **$12.95**

humanics

Post Office Box 7447
Atlanta, Georgia 30309

PROJECT IDEAS

416-80 AEROSPACE PROJECTS FOR YOUNG CHILDREN. Jane Caballero, Ph.D. This "first of it's kind" manual provides teachers and young students with an overview of aerospace history from kites and balloons, on to helicopters, gliders and airplanes, through todays satellites and the space shuttle. Each chapter is followed by interdisciplinary activities and field trip suggestions. **$12.95**

403-80 MATH MAGIC. Filled with ideas for creating a stimulating pre-school learning environment, this book encourages active participation in the learning process. Through songs, limericks, puzzles, games, and personal involvement it will help children become accustomed to basic math principles, such as classification, seriation, the development of logical thinking, as well as teaching them basic problem solving skills. Comes with "Magic Pouch" which contains full size games, puzzles, bulletin board aids and whimsical animals (17 x 24) as a supplement to the text. **$12.95**

Vol. I, 409-80, Vol. II, 410-80. WHEN I GROW UP. Michele Kavanaugh, Ph.D. Provides activities for expanding the human potential of male and female students, while eliminating sex-role stereotypes. Volume I contains experiences for pre-kindergarten thru 8th grade students. Volume II continues with input suitable for high school through young adulthood. **$10.95 ea.**

408-80 METRIC MAGIC. Kathy R. Thornburg, Ph.D. and James L. Thornburg, Ph.D. A fun book of creative classroom activities, *Metric Magic* was developed to teach preschoolers through sixth graders to think "metric." Includes action oriented activities involving the concept of length and progress through mass, area, volume, capacity, time, speed, and temperature. **$8.95**

417-80 ART PROJECTS FOR YOUNG CHILDREN. Jane Caballero, Ph.D. Over 100 stimulating projects for pre-school and elementary age children, including: drawing; painting; cut and paste; flannel and bulletin boards; puppets; clay; printing; textiles; and photography. Designed for those with limited budget and time schedule. Success oriented. $12.95

400-A CHILD'S PLAY. Barbara Trencher, M.S. A fun-filled activities and material book which goes from puppets and mobiles to poetry and songs, to creatively fill the pre-schoolers day. This handbook is a natural addition to a CDA or other competency-based learning program and has been used nation-wide for this purpose. $12.95

415-80 DESIGNING EDUCATIONAL MATERIALS FOR YOUNG CHILDREN. Jane Cabellero, Ph.D. A competency based approach providing over 125 illustrated activities encompassing language arts, health and safety, puppetry, math, and communication skills. Suggested functional areas and stated purpose for each activity make this a valuable tool for the CDA candidate. $14.95

PARENT INVOLVEMENT

419-80 FAMILY ENRICHMENT TRAINING. Gary Wilson and T. Thomas McMurrain. Designed for a workshop of six sessions, this program focuses on concerns for families today including communication, family relations, discipline, and developing self-esteem. Techniques such as role playing, small and large group interaction, and journals encourage participants to develop greater understanding of themselves and others. This package includes a manual for trainers, a participants "log" and the booklet "Dialog for Parents." $12.95

102-80 PARENTS AND TEACHERS. Gary B. Wilson. Offers strategies for staff trainers or anyone involved in parent or adult education. Included are training techniques which facilitate group interaction, team building, effective communication and self awareness. Designed to build a program promoting increased parent-staff interaction, each activity includes clear instructions, stated objectives, lists of materials and time requirements. $12.95

106-80 WORKING TOGETHER. Anthony J. Colleta, Ph.D. This practical handbook includes: plans for parent participation in the classroom; alternative approaches to teaching parenting skills; ideas for home based activities; and supplements to parent programs in the form of child development guides and checklists. $12.95

107-80 WORKING PARENTS. Susan Brown and Pat Kornhauser. Designed to make a positive impact on the family life of working parents, this book presents techniques which promote constructive and enjoyable parent-child interaction without disrupting the families daily routine. $12.95

24 Hour Direct Mail Service:
404·874·2176

420-80 BUILDING SUCCESSFUL PARENT-TEACHER PARTNERSHIPS. Kevin J. Swick, Ph.D., Carol F. Hobson, Ph.D. and R. Eleanor Duff, Ph.D. Deals with the issues of parent involvement by including: an in depth examination of the changing nature of parenting and teaching in recent decades — the emergence of the two-parent working family, the vanishing extended family, the one-parent working family, and a comprehensive plan for implementing successful parent-teacher programs. $10.00

ASSESSMENT

CD-507 CABS — CHILDREN ADAPTIVE SCALE. Bert O. Richmond and Richard H. Kicklighter. A testing tool for children ages 5-10 years. Created to measure skills in the following areas: (1) language development; (2) independent functioning; (3) family role performance; (4) economic-vocational activity and (5) socialization. Useful for enabling teachers to plan remediation for the child's level of adaptive behavior. Designed to be administered directly to the child.
Manual $14.95   Student Test Booklet $.65 ea.

ADOLESCENTS

411A-80 I LIVE HERE, TOO. Wanda Grey. Designed for the teacher who would like to improve the atmosphere in the classroom by helping each student to develop a more positive self concept. Themes such as "You Are One Of A Kind," "Know How You Feel," "You And Other People," "As Others See You," and "Using Your Creativity," will foster in children a better understanding of themselves and the people around them. $8.95

414S-80 H.E.L.P. FOR THE ADOLESCENT. Norma Banas, M.Ed. and J. H. Wills, M.S. Explores the underlying causes of the problems of the high school underachiever or potential dropout. Useful tests, programs and reading references are included to help identify "learning weaknesses" and promote "learning strengths." $ 6.95

humanics
Post Office Box 7447
Atlanta, Georgia 30309

SOCIAL SERVICES

302-80 ASSESSING STAFF DEVELOPMENT NEEDS. Gary B. Wilson, Gerald Pavloff and Larry Linkes. Provides a step-by-step methodology for determining the training needs of child development programs and planning their resolution. Tear-out worksheets and staff questionnaires will help clarify job descriptions and goal definitions, in conjunction with the needs assessment. $3.00

206-80 A SYSTEM FOR RECORD KEEPING. Gary B. Wilson, T. Thomas McMurrain and Barbara Trencher. Designed for family oriented social service agencies. This handbook is an integral part of HUMANICS Record Keeping System and should be used as a guide to proper use of the HUMANICS Record Keeping Forms. $12.95

201-80 INTERVENTION IN HUMAN CRISIS. T. Thomas McMurrain, Ph.D. Clearly presented intervention strategies based on an evaluation of crisis intensity and the response capacity of the individual or family. Rights, risks and responsibilities of the helper are also discussed. $6.95

MAINSTREAMING

404S-80 NEW APPROACHES TO SUCCESS IN THE CLASSROOM. Norma Banas, M.Ed. and J. A. Wills, M.S. A companion volume to Identifying Early Learning Gaps, designed for mainstream children in kindergarten through third grade. Includes activities structured to inspire the student who has experienced repeated failure and to help him or her acquire learning skills in the areas of reading, writing and arithmetic. Can be used in the classroom for the entire group or for a small group. $12.95

412S-80 LATON: THE PARENT BOOK. Mary Tom Riley, Ed.D. Presents a training plan for parents of handicapped children, designed to acquaint them with the resources, facilities, educational opportunities and diagnostic processes available to help them raise their children. This easy to read book will encourage parents to get involved. $12.95

New Publications

REALTALK: EXERCISES IN FRIENDSHIP AND HELPING SKILLS. George M. Gazda, Ed.D., William C. Childers, Ph.D., Richard P. Walters, Ph. D. A human relations training program for secondary school students including student text and instructor manual. REALTALK includes training in getting along with others, making and keeping friends, leadership, helping others deal with their problems and learning how to talk with practically anyone about practically anything.

THE LOLLYPOP TEST: A DIAGNOSTIC SCREENING TEST OF SCHOOL READINESS. Alex L. Chew, Ed.D. A lollypop loved by all. Children will enjoy taking this test for school readiness, educators will appreciate the easy quick, and significant results. Purpose of the test: (1) to assist the schools in identifying children needing additional readiness activities before entering first grade (2) to identify children with special problems and (3) to assist schools in planning individual and group instructional objectives. Culture-Free.

SPECIAL INTRODUCTORY PRICE $14.95 each

ORDER FORM

ORDER NO.	TITLE/DESCRIPTION	QUANTITY	PRICE

Subtotal . . . .

Ga. residents
add 4% sales tax . . . . .

Add shipping and
handling charges . . . . .

TOTAL . . . .

humanics

Make checks payable to:

HUMANICS LIMITED
P. O. Box 7447
Atlanta, Georgia 30309

Ship to:

NAME _____

ORGANIZATION _____

ADDRESS _____

CITY_____ STATE_____ ZIP_____

_____

(AREA CODE) TELEPHONE NO.

Institutional P.O. No._____

Date _____

Shipping and Handling Charges

Up to $10.00 add	$1.25
$10.01 to $20.00 add	$2.25
$20.01 to $40.00 add	$3.25
$40.01 to $70.00 add	$4.25
$70.01 to $100.00 add	$5.25
$100.01 to $125.00 add	$6.25
$125.01 to $150.00 add	$7.25
$150.01 to $175.00 add	$8.25
$175.01 to $200.00 add	$9.25

Orders over $200. vary depending
on method of shipment.

Printed in the United States
4223